Bible-Shaped
Teaching

Bible-Shaped
Teaching

John Shortt

WIPF *&* STOCK · Eugene, Oregon

Wipf & Stock
An Imprint of Wipf and Stock Publishers
199 W. 8th Ave., Suite 3
Eugene, OR 97401

www.wipfandstock.com

ISBN 13: 978-1-62564-558-6

Manufactured in the U.S.A.

For my grandsons, Callum and Dylan,
from whom and with whom I learn so much

Contents

Foreword

David I. Smith

PART OF BEING A Christian is to stand in, and to foster, a certain relationship to the Bible. Of the countless books imprinted on tablets, scrawled on papyrus, printed on paper, or downloaded to pocket devices since folk first began reading, this collection of writings holds a special place. It is to be received not just as a pleasant read, or a handy collection of information, or even a tool for inspiration. It offers itself to us as Scripture, as words given by God for us to ponder, think with, meditate upon, and obey. For Christians, the Bible is to play a significant role in shaping who we become.

Another part of being a Christian is to seek the kind of wholeness of life that the Bible calls for. "In all your ways acknowledge him, and he will make your paths straight," says the book of Proverbs in the Old Testament. "Offer your bodies as living sacrifices, holy and pleasing to God," says the book of Romans in the New Testament. These and various other passages point to a life that is not carved up into a religious zone that is kept for weekends but has little influence over how we conduct ourselves in the workplace or the marketplace. For Christians, life is to be approached as a whole.

For Christians who are teachers, these two simple (but challenging) truths can give rise to a particular kind of puzzlement. If our lives are to be consistently Christian, and the Bible is to direct our thinking and doing, and our calling is to teach, how do we connect these things together, especially when we find that the Bible has little or nothing directly to say about schools as they exist in the modern world or about many of the particular things that we teach? Could there be anything Christian or unchristian about how I teach mathematics, or languages, or biology? And is it any use drawing the Bible into such questions, when it is more concerned with salvation than with sums or cell systems?

This book offers help with such questions. It is not a how-to manual. It does not set out to provide a complete set of solutions or a Christian guide to every area of teaching and learning. Instead it focuses on understanding the different ways in which the Bible speaks, and on how we might build bridges between the world of the Bible and the world of today's classroom. It offers a map that shows some possible pathways towards being at one and the same time faithful to our calling as educators and faithful to the Scriptures as Christians.

Its author, John Shortt, has invested a lifetime in thinking about and helping other teachers to think about the craft of faithful Christian education. He is also himself a model Christian educator and a gentle, humble, winsome person. He is a fine choice of guide for those wanting to push a little further into questions about how the Bible might speak to teaching and learning. In the chapters that follow he sets out to broaden our sense of possibility—to free us from searching for the two or three verses that appear to say something about our discipline, and leave us instead with a wider sense of the variety of ways that that Bible can guide our paths.

How do stories (which make up much of the Bible) shape our sense of which ways to follow? How can the imagery of Scripture spark our educational imagination? What might we learn from the ways in which Jesus taught, or from the ways in which the Bible itself goes about teaching us? How do the truths stated in Scripture impinge on our beliefs about learning? What Christian virtues are important for teachers? These are big questions, deep questions, but in this book they are made accessible and brought alive through personal stories and examples. For any teacher looking to reflect further on how their accountability to Scripture might connect with their work in teaching, this book provides a valuable place to start.

Preface

THIS BOOK IS THE outcome of a long process of learning from and with many friends and colleagues, teachers, and students. It is an attempt to bring together insights gained from numerous personal conversations and classroom discussions as we have explored together ways in which the Bible shapes us in our lives and our work as teachers.

Two very good friends have especially influenced me in this process. One has been David Smith of the Kuyers Institute for Christian Teaching and Learning at Calvin College in the U.S. While we were colleagues in the research department of the Stapleford Centre in England, David and I worked together on a book entitled *The Bible and the Task of Teaching*. Most of the main ideas were David's and it was a great pleasure to work with him in the development of them. The book was written for a mainly academic readership of lecturers in college and university education departments, teachers studying for higher degrees in education, and others working at that level. It was published in 2002 and since then I have made much use of these ideas in working with teachers on courses and in conferences and seminars.

The other very good friend and key influencer has been Raymond Le Clair of the Center for Educational Programs in Kiev, Ukraine. I have learned much from Ray as we have travelled and worked together in conferences and on courses for teachers in Ukraine and Russia and elsewhere in that part of the world.

Together we have worked over the main ideas that I have been using in my presentations, refining them and adapting them for the school and classroom contexts in which these teachers work. In this process, the insights of these teachers have been invaluable and their enthusiasm and commitment to living for Christ in the classroom has been a constant encouragement and blessing.

Since the idea of writing this little book was born, both David and Ray have encouraged me to press on with it and provided detailed and very helpful comments on earlier drafts. Without their help and encouragement it would not have been completed, and I am very grateful to them for all they have done. I am also grateful to a number of other friends who made perceptive and helpful comments on later drafts. I am sure that the quality of the book has been enhanced by their input but the remaining inadequacies in it are undoubtedly all my own responsibility.

Although many of the key ideas in *The Bible and the Task of Teaching* are also present in this book, there are several significant differences between the two. In the first place, this book is intended for a wider readership and written in a more conversational style. I have made use of stories from my own childhood and teenage years, perhaps partly because I am at that stage in life where those early experiences and influences become more vividly present again but also because I heartily believe that, as teachers, we need to constantly endeavor to see things through the eyes of children and young people.

Secondly, in the earlier book David and I presented the links between the Bible and our work as classroom teachers (incarnation, statements, metaphors, story, and models) as intertwining strands of a rope. That has been replaced in this book by another metaphor: seeing the Bible as an environment that shapes us in various interrelated ways. One of the strands of the rope was incarnation, but that has been replaced here by embodiment and presented as an outcome of our being shaped by the Bible rather than as one of the ways in which it shapes us.

Thirdly, this book contains additional material in the form of an early chapter on the different ways in which we see and use the

Bible (chapter 2) and one towards the end on how biblical content can be used in a range of subjects in the classroom (chapter 8).

My prayer is that this book will prove helpful to many teachers as they seek to serve God in their work in the classroom and that they will refine and develop these ideas in their own reflective practice. Ultimately, it is all for him because, as Paul reminds us in Colossians 3:23–24, whatever we do, we are to work at it with all our hearts as working for him and not for others. It is the Lord Christ we are serving in our teaching. To him be praise and glory.

1

Life-Long and Life-Wide

THIS BOOK IS WRITTEN mainly for teachers but I am starting with a personal story from my early life and from a setting quite different from that of the classroom. I do this to show that the process of being shaped by the Bible is both life-long and life-wide.

Memories, Memories

I had been looking forward to this moment but now I hesitated. There, on a Dublin street outside an Italian restaurant, I paused briefly, knowing that what was to come would stimulate many memories and cause me to reflect on some of the changes that the years have brought.

Then I entered the restaurant. Most of the tables were empty so I was able to choose where I wanted to sit. Yes, this was the spot. This was where I had sat at my desk as a young man of seventeen when I started work in this very room in this very building, then the Irish headquarters of an international insurance company.

I ordered my meal and waited for it to come, memories flooding my mind. Nearly five decades had slipped into history since this young country boy, new to city life, had struggled to cope with the demands of work in a busy office where, it seemed, the phones never stopped ringing . . . and everybody else seemed so confident and knowing.

The main course arrived and I ate it slowly. People's names and faces came back with startling clarity. I looked around and remembered where their desks had been. There by the window sat James, my immediate superior, so quiet and patient. Patrick was a teenager like me; he had started work a few weeks before me but he was long accustomed to city life and seemed so self-assured. Bill was a big man whose desk was over to my right and, it has to be said, he was something of a bully. Anne had a very sharp tongue and would say some very unkind things with a sweet smile.

Tom was a smartly dressed man, an energetic person with reddish cheeks and always a smiling face. He was universally liked and related easily to everybody. Perhaps that was why he was the one who was charged by his colleagues to try to persuade me to join the trade union. In spite of his persuasiveness, I steadfastly refused to do this throughout the three years that I worked in that office building and even though (or, at least, so I was told) every other worker there was a member of the union.

Why the Lonely Stand?

Why did I take this lonely stand? If you had asked me then, I think I would have said that it was because I was a Christian and that becoming a member of the union would conflict with my faith.

To satisfy Tom (and my own inner questions), I had gone along to a union meeting. There were workers there from all the insurance companies in the city and they had hired a large meeting hall for the occasion. As it happened, it was a meeting hall owned by the YMCA and rented to the union for this meeting. A few months previously, at an after-church gathering for young people in the same hall, I had given my life to Jesus Christ. However, the atmosphere on this occasion was very different—no hymns and songs, no testimonies, no preacher, but instead a series of speakers who were all very negative in their denunciation of their employers and quite crude in their language. I observed . . . and I decided that this was not where a follower of Jesus Christ should be.

If you had pressed me further on the matter, I would probably have said that the Bible teaches that we should not be yoked together with unbelievers (2 Cor 6:14). I was determined to follow Christ and to be shaped by the Bible, and I was convinced that what the Bible taught applied to everything I was and did—not only to my life in church and in fellowship with other Christians.

Looking back from nearly half a century later, I still think that my concern was a godly one. I continue to be entirely convinced that it is right to seek to give the Bible a central place among all the influences that shape us and make us what we are and are becoming. However, I also think that in refusing to join the union I was not really being guided and shaped by the Bible as completely as I thought I was at the time. I was probably being shaped more by the influence of the self-employed Irish farmers among whom I had grown up, independent and self-made people who regarded trade union activity as the source of many of the problems with the country at the time. I was being shaped by a culture that saw people in authority as those who should always be respected and obeyed, and it seemingly did not occur to me that managers and company shareholders are, like the workers they employ, sinful beings and that they do not always hold their employees' best interests as a high priority.

In my reading of the Bible, I was failing to notice that the Lord Jesus, who I was rightly taking as the model for my living in the world, was one who kept company with the disreputable, the friend of sinners. I was insufficiently aware of the biblical concern for justice and fairness. I was not being sufficiently shaped by the biblical metaphors of salt and light that encourage us to be a transforming and illuminating influence in the world.

The Bible for All of Life

I have told this story because I believe that being shaped by the Bible is both life-long and life-wide. It is life-long in that it is important for us at every stage of life. I was a teenager who probably thought he had all the answers, but I was only just beginning. Years later, I am about to share with you some of what I've been learning since, both within the classroom and outside it, about how the Bible shapes us. However, in doing so I am very aware that I have so much more to learn, so much more to apply in my life and work.

Becoming Bible-shaped is also life-wide in that it is important in every kind of activity and in every context in which we find ourselves. This is a book written primarily for those who teach, and I shall seek to show in the chapters that follow how, in a variety of ways, the Bible shapes us as teachers. But not only as teachers, for I believe that these varied ways are relevant to us in whatever calling God puts us—healthcare, city planning, cab driving, advertising, IT project management, work in the arts or media, farming, and, yes, auto insurance . . . as well as school teaching. The Bible tells us that *whatever we do*, we are working for the Lord and it is him that we are serving (Col 3:23–24). Christian ministry is not confined to preaching, evangelism, and activity within the local church fellowship! We serve him wherever we are and wherever we work and we should be shaped by the Bible in and for all these contexts of our Christian service.

In this book we will be looking at different ways in which the Bible shapes us. (I should mention that here and throughout the book I am really talking about how God reveals himself and shapes us through the Bible.) The Bible comes to us in the form of a *story* and this has deep significance for how it may shape us. Bible *metaphors* have their place. So do the *statements* that the Bible makes and the *principles* that are expressed in or derived from these statements. The Bible provides us with *models* for our living.

How we expect the Bible to shape us depends on what kind of book we take it to be. So we will begin with this question: what kind of book is the Bible?

2

What Is the Bible Like?

WHAT KIND OF BOOK is the Bible? We use a range of metaphors to help us to understand what it is and how it affects our lives. At least one comes directly from the Bible and others are derived from what it says about itself.

What Kind of Light?

Psalm 119 has the line, "Your Word is a lamp for my feet, a light on my path" (v. 105). What kind of image comes to your mind as you read these words? Where are you in this mental picture? What are you doing? What kind of lamp is giving you light?

For my part, I am a young boy again on my parents' farm in rural Ireland in the 1950s. It is a dark moonless winter night and I am going out to the outhouse behind our house. I am carrying a lantern that gives enough light to see where I am walking but not much besides. No electricity on our farm in those days! The wind is blowing in the trees, unidentified sounds are coming at me from every direction, and I am desperately hoping that the flickering flame in the lantern will not be extinguished before I can get back to the warmth and safety of the living room.

The light the psalmist was talking about was surely more like that lantern than the bright streetlights of our modern cities. It would give enough illumination to see where we are putting our feet but not enough to see far into the distance on the way before us. An old hymn written nearly two hundred years ago by John Henry Newman has the same idea in its opening verse:

> Lead, kindly Light, amid th' encircling gloom, lead thou me on!
> The night is dark, and I am far from home; lead thou me on!
> Keep thou my feet; I do not ask to see
> The distant scene; one step enough for me.

Is this how you think about the Bible and the role it should play in your daily life? A light that shows you the next few steps but not the whole way ahead? Or do you think of a bright city light that banishes the darkness in all directions? The former is surely more true to the context of Psalm 119 than the latter.

Some Other Popular Images

Another very influential metaphor derived from the Bible is that of the foundations of a building. A popular hymn applies it to the Bible itself in describing it as being like a "firm foundation" for the "saints of the Lord." In similar ways, Christians often talk of "biblical foundations" and see the Bible as that upon which we seek to build our lives. The image is probably less common in the Bible than it is in our talk and, where it is used in the Bible, it seems to refer more to the person of Jesus Christ as the foundation or cornerstone than to the Bible or what it says.

Rather than a light or a foundation, we sometimes see the Bible as being like a roadmap or a satellite navigation system for a journey, or an instruction handbook for the maintenance and use of a piece of equipment. Viewing the Bible like this makes it essentially a source of information that we need. It is a common image according to which the Bible tells us what we need to know, and not just for the next step or the next day but probably for more than that.

Some people take this image much further in seeing the Bible as a source of information on every conceivable subject matter. It is not simply a source of what we *need* but of information on everything that we could ever *want* to know about. For those who see it this way, the Bible is like an encyclopaedia. Roy Clouser terms this the "encyclopaedic assumption" in his helpful book *The Myth of Religious Neutrality*.[1] It is an assumption that he questions, and I think rightly so, because it undervalues the role of God's general revelation in the wonderful world he has made, whereby, as Paul says, "God's invisible qualities" may be "understood from what has been made" (Rom 1:20).

Another influential image for the Bible is that of a pair of spectacles through which we view the world. John Calvin used this image in chapter 6 of his *Institutes of the Christian Religion* and many have followed his lead. Talk of "world*views*" and "perspectives" is closely linked with it.

Many more metaphors are possible. In his helpful book *Holy Bible, Human Bible*, Gordon Oliver likens it to, among other things, an open window through which wonderful things are seen, a conversation partner, and a strange country to be explored by us as today's foreigner-citizens. Richard Briggs,' in his book *Reading the Bible Wisely*, suggests we should see the Bible not as a compass or chart for our voyage but as directions to find the Pilot.[2]

How About This One?

All these metaphors are helpful and all also have their limitations. Different ones bring to the foreground different aspects of the role that the Bible plays in our lives and even different roles that we think it could or ought to play. They also tend to suggest different roles for us in relation to the Bible. Seeing the Bible as providing foundations for a building gives us an active role in working on the basis of what is fixed and settled. Images like spectacles or

1. Clouser, *The Myth of Religious Neutrality*, 94
2. Briggs, *Reading the Bible Wisely*, 92.

windows leave us in a more spectatorial role. We are watching the game being played on the field rather than actively participating in it. Thinking of maps, instruction manuals, or an encyclopaedia brings to the foreground a particular aspect of our activity—our reasoning processes.

In this book I am discussing the ways the Bible shapes us as people and, in particular, as teachers in the classroom. I have been wondering which image best fits that shaping role. Talk of shaping could suggest that we are passive, that we are shaped in spite of ourselves, but I've been searching for an image that gives more place to our thought and activity because that, I think, fits well with how the Bible presents this shaping process. Perhaps you can think of a better one but, in the meantime, please join me in thinking of the Bible as being like a new environment in which we find ourselves, a new ecology in which we live and move and have our being.

Imagine that you have found yourself on a remote Pacific island (or a village in rural Africa, or a town by a Norwegian fiord, or some such place that is new to you). Different aspects of this new environment will affect you as a person and influence what you do to adapt to it and to learn to live in it. The climate, terrain, vegetation, people, their language and culture, modes of transport, food and how it is obtained, houses, animals, birds, and other wildlife are all different from what you are accustomed to.

Some effects will be experienced subconsciously and others will involve your conscious thought and planning. To an extent, you will be able to think about them as distinct influences but, at the same time, they are interrelated and working together to make you a different person.

The local people will introduce you to aspects of your environment of which you have only been vaguely aware. You will learn to notice them and read them for yourself, e.g., the signs of the weather in the clouds, the wind, and the behavior of the birds and animals, or the presence of plants that have particular healing properties. Not only will you notice things you had not noticed before (as an avid bird watcher, I am amazed at people who do not even seem to see or hear the birds around them!) but you will also make changes in your life under their influence.

The Bible is an environment that we should seek to inhabit, and in which to live and breathe. It is an environment that shapes us in different and interrelated ways. Some of these we may never have noticed before or have but a vague sense of their influence. Others we may be more familiar with but we may not realize how influential they actually are or can be. We may be too preoccupied with some and fail to see how they form part of a larger whole—like the novel foods on the island that are prepared and eaten according to local customs and form part of a whole process of hunting or cultivation.

In this book we will be looking one by one at several ways in which the Bible environment influences us as people and as teachers in the classroom, but let us be aware that they, like the influences of a whole new environment, are interrelated in a complex whole.

1. What mental images do you have of the Bible and the role it plays in your life? In your teaching?

2. How do these metaphors resonate with how the Bible refers to itself and the images it uses of itself?

3. Can you think of any differences it would make in our lives and relationships if we thought of the Bible as an environment in which we live and breathe? How would it affect our teaching?

3

The Power of the Narrative

THE FIRST OF THE ways in which the Bible shapes us and our classroom teaching is related to the story that it tells. We therefore come now to the topic of stories and those big worldview stories that we call metanarratives.

Stories, Stories Everywhere

My little three-year-old grandson, Callum, climbed on my knee with one of his favorite storybooks. I read a bit and then, from his memory of the many times we had done this before, he told the next bit . . . and on we went together, telling the story in turns to each other. However, this time was to be different for, when we got to the last page, one of us (I can't remember which) turned over to the blank page at the end and the blank inside cover of the book and we continued the story together, telling each other what might have happened next. The pictures in the inward eye were much more vivid than those on the earlier printed pages as we went forward together in our imaginations.

We all enjoy stories. As children we love them, but as adults too are we not also easily caught up in stories we read, hear, or view on screen? Those novels for bedtime or vacation reading, the detective mystery unfolding on TV, the blog of that friend's travels on the Internet, the heart-to-heart sharing of a life's ups and downs by a complete stranger sitting beside us on a long bus journey. They have different settings, different plot lines, different characters and themes, different lengths. We listen to them, we read them, we view them in plays and films, we hear them in song, we make them up, we tell them. They make us laugh, cry, reflect, imagine, lose ourselves—as my grandson and I did in that tale that we read together.

Little Callum is now eight years old and we will shortly be all together on a family vacation on the farm in Ireland where I was brought up—my wife and I, our son and daughter-in-law, and Callum and his little brother, Dylan. I wonder what the Irish weather will be like and what the going will be like underfoot. If both are good, I could take the boys on a walk in the footsteps of another old man and another little boy.

I was that little boy nearly six decades ago. The old man was Reverend Kenny, a visitor to our home who was in the area because he was leading a mission in the little country church where we worshipped as a family. I had been given the responsibility of taking Reverend Kenny on a tour of the farm. He was ancient and white-haired and he walked slowly and stiffly so I had to slow down for him.

I showed him the prehistoric monument that was hidden from view among some trees. This was a dolmen, a table-shaped stone structure with a very large flat rock laid on top of several small upright ones. My brothers and I knew it as "the Big Rock." The ancient visitor evidenced interest in this much more ancient monument, but not for very long. We walked a little distance further among the trees. Reverend Kenny stopped and pointed at a tree that lay dead on the ground. The tree had thick tendrils of ivy twined around it, as thick as a man's arm.

"John," Reverend Kenny said, "Do you see the ivy on this dead tree, how it has grown up around the tree and choked it and eventually brought it crashing to the ground?" I nodded my head respectfully—for adults were always right and white-haired gentlemen wearing clerical collars (as Reverend Kenny did) knew everything there was to know that was of any importance. "Sin is like that ivy," Reverend Kenny continued, "It climbs up around us as we grow older and, if we do nothing about it, it can ruin our lives, choke us, and kill us."

I can't remember what happened next. The walk back to the thatched farmhouse? The tea probably, with hot buttered scones and the best cups and plates? The conversation around the table? The visitor's departure? I cannot remember any of that but I have never forgotten Reverend Kenny's words about sin. It is as if it happened yesterday. In a moment I am back there among the trees near the Big Rock, looking down at the ivy on a dead tree. "Sin is like that" are the words I hear ringing down through the decades.

Yes, perhaps I *will* take Callum and Dylan for a walk together into that story!

We Think and Dream in Stories

Stories are central to the way in which we structure our understanding of ourselves and others, and of actions and events. They are part of our language and thought, of our whole experience of the world and our way of living.

We don't just enjoy them as diversions; we *think* in stories. And we dream in stories, however chaotic these tales of the night may be at times. Whether waking or sleeping, we place characters and events in patterns in space and time. We locate ourselves and one another and the things that happen to us and around us in narrative contexts.

We are story makers! Whether listening on the train to half a conversation that somebody is having on his cell phone, or reading the inscriptions on gravestones, or anticipating the next episode of a serial story on the radio, we cannot help filling in the details. There is a fundamental incompleteness to all the stories that we tell, just as Callum and I experienced when we came to the blank pages at the end of his storybook and found that we just had to continue the story.

The writer Alasdair MacIntyre shows how we need context to understand a story. He invites you to imagine that you are standing by a bus stop. A young man is standing next to you, also waiting for a bus. Although he is a complete stranger, he suddenly turns to speak to you and says, "The name of the common wild duck is *Histrionicus histrionicus histrionicus.*" You guess that the three repeated words must form the Latin name for the wild duck and you know the meaning of the other words in his sentence. However, you have no idea of what he meant in the sense of what he was doing in saying this to you. MacIntyre goes on to suggest scenarios that would make the stranger's utterance meaningful:

> He has mistaken me for someone who yesterday had approached him in the library and asked: "Do you by any chance know the Latin name of the common wild duck?" Or he has just come from a session with his psychotherapist who has urged him to break down his shyness by talking to strangers. "But what shall I say?" "Oh, anything at all." Or he is a Soviet spy waiting at a prearranged rendezvous and uttering the ill-chosen code sentence which will identify him to his contact. In each case, the act of utterance becomes intelligible by finding its place in a narrative.[1]

I was once relating MacIntyre's story to a group of teachers when one of them suggested another possible scenario: the young stranger was preparing for his biology examination!

We need the story context in order to understand a sentence. A sentence is not fully meaningful on its own. We need a context to see the point of uttering it. In a similar way, words may have a range of meanings given in a dictionary, but the use of a word is not meaningful without the context of the sentence in which it is placed.

A word needs the context of a sentence, a sentence needs the context of a story and, as little Callum and I found that day, a story calls for the wider context of a bigger and more complete story.

1. MacIntyre, *After Virtue*, 210.

This is true of our own personal stories, the stories of our lives. They too need the context of bigger stories to make sense of them.

Our life stories are special to us for, as a T-shirt slogan has it, "I am starring in my own soap opera!" Some details we can't remember. Some we remember fuzzily. Some we remember with clarity as if they had happened yesterday. Some we will never forget as long as we have our faculties—as with me and my memory of Reverend Kenny teaching me as an eight-year-old boy about the effects of sin.[2]

We locate ourselves in the stories of our lives, stories with a beginning at which we were present but cannot remember and an end which we know will surely come but we cannot usually anticipate how it will be. Other people are actors in our stories and, as we soon begin to realize, they have their own stories in which we are also actors. When two people meet, two life stories meet and overlap.

This is of particular importance to us as teachers whose working lives are all about meeting with others, children and young people, with whose life stories ours overlap. In his book *The Courage to Teach*, Parker Palmer quotes from Martin Buber: "All real living is meeting"—and he adds, "And teaching is endless meeting."[3] How true, how very true!

Not only are there stories all about us—our stories and those of other people meeting, interacting, overlapping, and developing day by day—but we find that these our stories are parts of bigger stories, stories of communities and traditions, of people and races.

---

2. I have often told this story through the years, but with no more knowledge of this man than that he was a clergyman who had led a mission at Easter that year in the little church where my family worshipped, and that he had walked and talked with me that day. It was therefore very moving in the course of revising the manuscript of this book to find a reference to him on the website of the Irish Church Missions, and not surprising to read that Revd. William Edward Kenny was there described as "a man of extensive scholarship and deep evangelical convictions."

3. Palmer, *Courage to Teach*, 16.

My little story from childhood is part of the bigger story of my life which is still being written. It in its turn is part of bigger stories. They are part of history. Reverend Kenny and I were looking together at a dolmen that had a story going back so far that we call it prehistory!

We (and those we teach) make sense of life, sense of our own lives, by locating them in the big worldview stories that we call metanarratives. They provide the larger context for us to understand what it is all about.

We Need Metanarratives

There are many worldview stories. Each of them encapsulates basic beliefs about the way the world works. They directly and indirectly shape the way we think and live.

There is, for example, the metanarrative of human beings all on their own in a chance universe, working their way up from nothingness, ever making progress in their understanding, needing no power beyond themselves. Life is getting better all the time as we learn more and can do more. But is this story true? Yes, we know and understand many things that our ancestors didn't. Our mobile technology gives us instant communication across thousands of miles even when we are out walking on a mountain slope. Our medical techniques save us from illnesses of which people lived in fear even a few decades ago. A few clicks on the computer keyboard give us access to masses of information formerly stored on many miles of library shelving. But is life really getting better in all respects? Are we human beings on our own making progress towards perfect harmony in our relationships, mastering our selfish impulses and finding a way of coping with the inner despairs and dreads that haunt us in the dark hours? I suggest not. But that's a story in which many people live and move and have their being, the story of the "Ascent of Man," the story of optimistic humanism.

Neil Postman, in his book *The End of Education*, lists the following as some of the stories in which people lived in late twentieth-century North America: Reason, Scientism, Consumerism,

Economic Utility, Tribalism or Separatism, and Information Technology.[4]

Postman goes on to suggest how some of these big stories can be embedded in the little stories that we read, tell, and dream about. His particular and striking example of this is in the stories told to us and, over and over again, to our impressionable young children in the thousands of TV advertisements that are beamed into our homes and the inner rooms of our thoughts and imaginations. He says that they are like religious parables. They tell us what is wrong with us and our lives, and they go on to tell us the way out of our problems, the way of salvation, and then they show how we will live happily ever after in a paradise world.[5] For example, we are not using the right kind of knives in the kitchen so family meal times are very unhappy. We buy the right knives and we can cut our meat so easily and now life is wonderful. Or we are boys whom the girls do not seem to find attractive. We buy the right deodorant and suddenly everything is different. Life is perfect forever afterwards!

The big story embedded in these little stories is that buying things makes us happy. It is the big story of Consumerism that Postman sums up succinctly and starkly as: "He who dies with the most toys wins."[6] For many, including many of our young people, this big story has supplanted the humanist big story of Reason.

The Big True Story of God

What great story is adequate to provide a true and meaning-giving context to the stories of our lives? Surely it must be the Greatest Story of all stories! This is a story that is bigger than all of us. This is the Big True Story of God, the Christian metanarrative. There are lots of stories in the Bible but they are all set in the context of a big story that begins with God himself. He made everything. He

4. Postman, *End of Education*, chs. 2–3.

5. Ibid., 33–35.

6. Ibid., 33.

made us. But we disobeyed him and we chose to go our own way. As a result, we were sent out of his beautiful garden, no longer able to walk and talk with him as his children.

The focal point of this story is the death and resurrection of Jesus. The cross is the hinge of history and the body of Jesus was broken on that hinge. But we come through to the other side—to life that shall never end! Death is not the end because death itself is defeated by the one who came back from death and will never die.

He will return and make everything new. There will be "a new heaven and a new earth, where righteousness dwells" (2 Pet 3:13). The kingdom of God is here already, it is within us, but it is also still to come.

This is not only a story of what happened in the past. It tells of what will happen in the future. The best is yet to come! But it is not only a story of the past and of the future, it is a story of what is happening now!

The Bible comes to us not in the form of a textbook of theology but as a narrative, as the Big True (and amazing) Story of God and his world. The form is primarily that of a story, and even where it isn't the context of its poems and letters is still that Big Story of God and the world he has made, the world of people like you and me. Even our statements of belief in our creeds are retellings of this story, of movements of characters and events in space and time.

1. What big cultural stories shaped you as you grew up and exerted their influence in your life and thoughts as a child? As a teenager? As a college or university student?

2. What did you dream about being when you grew up and what stories pervaded those dreams?

3. What do you dream about now and what stories are shaping those dreams?

4

Living and Teaching in the Big Story

Stepping into the Big Story

Bryan, a teacher from Australia, tells of some teenagers encountering this story:

> It happened in a classroom seven years ago. . . . Over the preceding twelve weeks, my Year 9 Christian Studies class had been reading and "studying" Mark's Gospel. These fourteen- and fifteen-year-old boys and girls were not a particularly religious group. Of the twenty-four in the class, only four came from a family which had any association with a Christian church.
>
> Inspired in part by Philip Yancey's book *The Jesus I Never Knew*, I had invited the students to assume the persona of first century journalist covering the life of Jesus from Mark 1 through to chapter 16. Their task was to file multiple stories based on imaginary interviews conducted with Jesus, each of his disciples and with each of the individuals and representatives of the groups he encountered.
>
> With two fifty-five minute lessons each week, we had action-filled twelve weeks. Every student remained engaged with the gospel. They learned much about the customs of the people whom Jesus met; they were, at times, astounded by the way Jesus spoke to some people. But it was their very frank and unflattering assessment

of Jesus' disciples that I remember most clearly. Thinking that Mark might have had a prejudiced view towards them, they dipped into the accounts given by Luke, John and Matthew to see if there was not another side to their character, behaviour and evidence of learning. "Why are they so stupid?" some asked. "If Jesus has told them once, he's told them a dozen times who he is and what he is about, but they still can't get it and want to squabble amongst themselves as to which of them is or will be the greatest."

So when it came to Peter's denial of Jesus just prior to his crucifixion, they were beside themselves in amazement and disappointment at how he could be so cowardly and double-faced.[1]

Bryan goes on to comment that his teenage students left Mark's Gospel with many positive insights into the person of Jesus, but also with not too complimentary a view of the disciples, especially Peter and Judas. They then moved on together to the Acts of the Apostles. Bryan continues the story:

This time I decided to use the great speeches (though a more conventional teacher might refer to them as sermons) as the vehicle through which to learn how the gospel was spread after Jesus' resurrection and ascension. I decided to do a dramatic reading of Peter's speech in Acts 2 using JB Phillips' paraphrase. The students listened attentively. Indeed this was the most attentive they had ever been. At the end of the final sentence there was absolute silence. It was as if we were reliving the actual event—till one boy raised his hand and exclaimed, "Surely this is not the same Peter we encountered in Mark's gospel!" To which another four or five students added, "He's a new person . . . his life has been changed . . . do you think, Sir, that the resurrection of Jesus might have led to this . . . or was it the coming of God's Spirit?"

If ever there was an "aha!" moment, surely this was it![2]

1. See Shortt, "This Was a Real 'Aha!' Moment."
2. Ibid.

Bryan has told us of teenagers encountering God's Big Story for the first time. Stepping into it as strangers, the wonder of it all was dawning upon them. For many of us who have been steeped in the Bible's stories for as long as we can remember, their familiarity can prevent us from experiencing this wonder. Perhaps we need to step into them as if doing so for the very first time.

An Important Interlude:
Meeting an Objection to All This Talk of Story

But, you may well be saying by now, doesn't all this talk of story suggest that the Bible is not true, that it is a work of fiction? And doesn't talk of "stepping into the story" suggest that what we do is all make-believe? If that is your response, I know what it feels like, for it was also my response when I first heard people talk of the story of the Bible. But I came to realize that stories are not necessarily fictional! Your biography, the story of your life, is surely a true story. History is narrative, it is story, but that does not mean it is a work of fiction. In an old hymn, we call on one another to tell us "the old, old story . . . of Jesus and his love." In the 1960s, people flocked to see a film about the life of Jesus entitled *The Greatest Story Ever Told*. Stories may be fictitious but they do not have to be so. And when I talk of God's Big Story, please, please remember that I am talking of it as a *true* story and not as a fictional account.

Living in God's Big True Story

We saw earlier that the storyline of the Bible includes the present time and the future to come. It therefore includes our time and us so we are not spectators but players. We are in Acts 29 (the ongoing chapter that follows the last one in the New Testament book of that name). Being shaped by the Bible story involves our stepping into it and indwelling it. In his 2009 lecture at the inauguration of Wheaton College's new Center for Early Christian Studies, Dr. R. L. Wilken said this:

It is not enough to say that Christ was crucified. One
must say with Saint Paul, "I am crucified with Christ."
Likewise it is not enough to say, "Christ is raised." One
who knows Christ says, "We shall also live with Him."[3]

Bryan's students were, for the most part, encountering the
story of the life, death, and resurrection of Jesus for the first time.
For at least a short time, they were living in the story. They had
stepped into the story. They were walking in it. But, of course, the
experience could be a passing one. They could step back out again,
like football players brought off the field of play by their coaches
and returned to the spectatorial position of the substitutes bench,
or members of a daytime cinema audience emerging blinking into
the full light of day.

In the Sunday morning service, the mid-week home group
Bible study, or the family prayers we may see ourselves as living
in the Big True Story of God who is active in the world that he
has made and not forgotten. But what of the geography lesson on
Monday morning, the playground supervision, the private session
with the problem student, the staff meeting after school on Friday?
Living in the story goes deeper than merely thinking about or telling the stories—either the stories of the Bible or the many little
stories in which God's story may be embedded. It is not merely
living *as if* it were true but living in it *because* it is true, it is how
things really are in time and history.

In a ground-breaking paper entitled "How Can the Bible Be
Authoritative?," Tom Wright proposes that we should understand
the authority of the Bible not so much as a matter of following
rules but rather as one of dramatic improvisation.

He invites us to see the Bible as being like acts 1–4 of an un-
finished play by William Shakespeare. It also provides some detail
of how the play will finally work out. But act 5 is missing and we
are called, like Shakespearean actors, to immerse ourselves thor-
oughly in acts 1–4 and what we can discern of the final outcome so
that we can construct together the missing act in ways that are as
consistent as we can make them with the rest of the play.

3. Wilken, "Going Deeper into the Bible."

We are improvising but it is not a case of simply making it up as we go along, still less a case of "anything goes." Yes, there is indeed place for our human imagination and creativity but, at the same time, we should faithfully seek to be true to the intentions of the author and together produce an act 5 that is consistent with the story so far. This gives room for creativity as we seek to live in God's story, but it is always within constraints. There is always the need for consistency and careful thinking. Different groups of actors may come with different versions of act 5, and the same group may do so at different times and in different places, but all alike in their diversity are called to show faithfulness and consistency with the author's intentions as shown in what he has given to them.

It is not so much a matter of telling a story in our words or our lives as of stepping into it and inviting others to step into it with us so as to experience together what it is to be in God's story.

Teaching in God's Big True Story

All of this has significance for how we live and how we teach.

Firstly, it changes how we view other people, including the children and young people in our classrooms or youth clubs. When two people meet, it is not a matter of two objects being together at the same time and in the same place. Rather, what we have is two life stories coming together, overlapping, and, for a time short or long, flowing along side by side. Those we teach are also, as the T-shirt slogan said, starring in their own soap operas. They bring into the teaching and learning situation their own joys and sorrows, despairs and hopes, memories good and bad. Relating to a person is not simply relating to a personality as it is at the moment, but to a whole life history. For a short or longer time, we walk along with them and, if we are truly living in God's Big Story, we hope that this will show itself in how we walk and talk, how we relate together.

Secondly, because this is a story that we take to be true and filled with a bright prospect for the future, we should be characterized by hope. A hymn that paraphrases a prayer of Francis of Assisi has the line, "Where there's despair, let me bring hope." We expect a bright tomorrow, so living in this story should make us a hopeful people. People filled with hope live differently, teach and learn differently, from those who cannot see much beyond the present.

Thirdly, if stories, big and little, are so important to human living, we will *tell* stories. Jesus the Great Teacher told lots and lots of stories to adults and surely also to children and young people. Can we be satisfied with teaching that is full of abstractions with few concrete ties to everyday life? Stories immerse us and our students in the real and ordinary everyday world, God's world for which we are to care and in which we are called to serve. This is quite different from the all-too-common practice of using biblical and other stories simply as a way of getting across a "moral."

The use of stories can humanize our teaching of subjects like mathematics.[4] For example, the study of networks can be brought down to earth by looking at the historical problem of finding a walk across the seven bridges of Königsburg (now Kaliningrad) that would cross each bridge once and only once. Leonhard Euler's proof in 1735 that such a walk was impossible has led to the development of network theory, with applications from physics and chemistry to sociology, and has helped to make possible the Internet in our time. And all because some residents in an eighteenth-century European city were asking what may seem to us now a fairly pointless question!

The life stories of scientists and mathematicians can also be a rich source for relating these subjects to the lives of human beings in God's world. It is said that Georg Cantor, best known as the originator of the theory of sets in mathematics, wanted to understand the mathematical idea of infinity better because of a concern with understanding better what it meant to say that God is infinite. The life-stories of musicians, artists, poets and others can also give evidence of their desire to understand and portray God and his world.

4. There is a very helpful book entitled *Teaching as Story Telling* by Kieran Egan in which he writes of the importance of imagination and the place of stories in the teaching of all subjects.

Fourthly, we need to be aware of the big stories that may be embedded in the little stories that we tell and the examples that we use in our teaching. Taking an example again from mathematics (because it is the subject where stories would at first sight seem to be out of place!): teaching percentages by referring repeatedly to the interest *we* receive from investments can promote the consumerist big story that says it is more blessed to receive than to give. A unit in a Charis Project's mathematics book in the UK countered this by relating percentages not to interest received but to the benefit given to a charity through it's receiving from the government the tax that would have been paid by the donor on the amount of his gift.[5] A focus on story means that we need to ensure that both the big stories we literally tell in our words and those that we tell in the way we live are consistent with the biblical Big True Story.

Fifthly, we need to be always discerning what story we are really, in practice, indwelling. Although we may regard ourselves as living in the biblical story, reflection on our daily lives may lead us to conclude that most of the time we are actually living as if an alternative big story were true, e.g., the humanist story of upward progress or the consumerist story of how "retail therapy" can cure all our ills. In this reflective process, to change the image for a moment to the popular one of foundations, we are more like archaeologists than builders: we are digging down to find the foundations on which our lives are actually being lived rather than laying foundations and building on them.

Sixthly and surely most importantly of all, we need to be immersed in the Bible and its Big Story, not simply as a book about long ago and far away but as a book about yesterday, today, and forever. For this, I suggest that we need to be looking for new ways of reading and hearing the Bible. I am struck by how, in the story told by Bryan from Australia, it was hearing a dramatic reading of Peter's speech that had such an impact on his students. Too often in our churches, the Bible reading is a preface to the "real business" of the sermon rather than a listening to God speaking through it.

5. Shortt and Westwell, *Charis Mathematics*, 31–37.

Immersion in the biblical story means that, as Gordon Oliver puts it, we "live with integrity in this 'time between the times' . . . [for we are] called to live on the doorstep of something that is about to happen and to find ways of holding the door open so that it can start to happen now."[6]

A narrative focus on living in God's story is one of the interrelated, overlapping, and mutually supporting ways in which we can be shaped by the environment of the Bible. Metaphor provides another way and to this we turn in the next chapter.

1. What might an emphasis on story mean for what and how we teach?

2. What might it mean for our choices of the stories that we use and for how we use them? How might we handle the big stories that may be embedded in them?

3. Are the big stories in your life different from the stories that are being formed in your students by your contemporary society? If so, how should that influence your teaching?

6. Oliver, *Holy Bible, Human Bible*, 77.

5

Metaphors We Live and Teach By

IN THE LAST TWO chapters, we have been looking at stories and the shaping influence on our lives and teaching of living in God's story. We turn now to the shaping influence of metaphors.

We Live by Metaphors

Not only is the shaping environment of the Bible in which we are called to live and teach thickly populated by stories, it is also replete with metaphors. Jesus, the Great Teacher, was not only a great storyteller, he was also a painter of vivid pictures in the mind through his use of metaphors. The Good Shepherd whose sheep follow him, the Vine of whom we are the branches, the Living Bread from heaven . . . and many, many more have shaped us and continue to do so.

Nearly six decades ago, Reverend Kenny told me, as we stood together by the fallen tree near the Big Rock, that sin is like the ivy that took a stranglehold of the tree and brought it crashing to the ground. That image lives with me still. He taught me much in that single sentence and its word picture. His metaphor was not itself taken from the Bible but it wonderfully brought together the biblical metaphors that portray sin as both a heavy weight and a form of slavery.[1]

Barbara is a Christian teacher from England who tells this story:

> At a conference, a speaker held up a transparent plastic cube made up of compartments arranged in a sort of maze. There were small openings between compartments through which a small ball bearing could pass. It was an illustration of the school curriculum and the parts making up the whole. He then showed us a living sponge with each part growing from and into the other. "This is what the curriculum should be like," he said quietly and almost wistfully, "Organically connected and exciting." I realized that if the curriculum was an expression of God's integrated creation, it could begin to be everything the speaker longed for it to be.
>
> From that moment over twenty years ago I have enjoyed and explored the creativity involved in the whole process of curriculum design.[2]

Barbara's story gives us another example of the shaping power of metaphor. For her, replacing the more static image for the curriculum of interconnected compartments with the living dynamic one of a sponge helped her to see and do things differently.

Here I am taking metaphor to be, as Janet Soskice has put it, "that figure of speech whereby we speak about one thing in terms which are seen to be suggestive of another."[3] It is a case of "seeing as" (rather than simply "seeing") which can deepen our understanding and enhance our practice.

We have already seen something of the role of metaphors when in chapter 2 we were considering how we view and use the Bible (light, roadmap, foundation, etc.). In that chapter, I assumed the importance of metaphor for our understanding. However,

---

1. In his book *Sin: A History*, Gary Anderson writes about the different metaphors that the Bible uses for sin and he argues that how we talk about sin influences deeply what we do about it.

2. See Shortt, "This Was a Real 'Aha!' Moment."

3. Soskice, *Metaphor and Religious Language*, 15.

metaphors, like stories, are often viewed as something decorative but not really necessary in human living and understanding. Against this, many would nowadays argue that metaphors, in the words of David Smith, are "not water-lilies on a pond, decorative and opaque" but rather "windows through which the light of a particular vision of reality is refracted."[4]

In their book with the significant title *Metaphors We Live By*, George Lakoff and Mark Johnson point out that in our Western cultural contexts we think of argument as if it were a form of warfare (we "win," "lose," "attack," and "defend" arguments). How different things would be, they say, if we were to think of argument as a form of dance, i.e., a cooperative, turn-taking activity that moves to a mutually satisfying conclusion.

To take another example, the language we use about time treats it as a scarce commodity like money (we "waste," "spend," and "lose" time and we may have time "to spare"). This is very different from the way rural peoples in Africa generally view time. For them, it seems that when God made time he made plenty of it, and they tell us that we have the clocks and watches but they have the time—time to think, time to talk, time for people rather than programs of activity.

The metaphors we use are embedded in our ways of seeing the world, our worldviews. They can also themselves generate new ways of seeing things that in turn enable us to do things in new ways and lead to advances in our understanding. Coming to see the heart as a pump or the brain as a telephone exchange—impossible before the invention of pumps and telephones—led to advances in medical science. Coming to see light as both wave and particle or electricity as current led to advances in physical science.

In an article about the role of these "generative metaphors,"[5] Donald Schön provides an example from the world of paintbrush manufacture. Brushes were being made with synthetic bristles, but compared with the old natural-bristle brushes the new ones delivered paint to a surface in a way that was not smooth and

---

4. Smith and Shortt, *Bible and the Task of Teaching*, 120.

5 Schön, "Generative Metaphor."

continuous. The designers tried a range of approaches but without success until one of them suggested that they try seeing a paintbrush as a kind of pump. This led them to focus attention on the spaces between the bristles and led to a solution of their problem.

Not all new metaphors lead to helpful developments; some can lead in the opposite direction and could be described as degenerative. Paulo Freire, the Brazilian Christian educator, in his classic work *Pedagogy of the Oppressed*, argues against what he terms the banking idea of teaching whereby we see ourselves as depositors and our students as depositories who receive, file, and store what we deposit within their memory banks. Seeing education as an assembly line process is also, many would argue, degenerative and indeed dehumanizing.

Metaphors often come in clusters or networks, each with its own root or core metaphor, e.g., argument as warfare or time as money. These metaphor clusters inhabit our ways of thinking and influence our attitudes and actions. With changed ways of thinking come changed networks of metaphor. For example, recent years have seen metaphors that had their traditional home in the marketplace coming to influence education and other areas, e.g., healthcare, as we increasingly talk of the "products" of education, of pupils or parents as "clients" or "customers," of "delivery" of the curriculum and of "quality control" of the process. These new networks of imagery both reflect changed ways of thinking and doing things and, in their turn, they reinforce, sustain, and even help to create these changes.

Military metaphors can also be unhelpful. Students may be referred to as "troops," teachers work "in the trenches," and teaching is reduced to "strategy." Such clusters of metaphors tend to promote a competitive, combative atmosphere in a school.

We are right to regard this as a negative development but, at the same time, we should welcome the more positive development of the biblical language of mission and vision, or of leader-as-servant becoming commonplace in education and in the marketplace.

Metaphors We Teach By

I've asked groups of teachers and student teachers many times for their metaphors for teaching.[6] Here are some of the images they have come up with: orchestra conductor, sports coach, mountain guide, parent, and gardener. One student said he saw himself as a drum circle leader, the facilitator who sets the beat for a circle of drummers and percussionists. Another saw herself as being like a parent giraffe that brings the high branches down low enough for the young giraffes to browse.

All of these are positive images of the teacher, but some of us have known teachers who must have seen themselves as army sergeants and others who were clearly enjoying themselves as actors in center stage!

The writer Kieran Egan asks us to see ourselves as storytellers. Samson Makhado from South Africa has written an article in which he talks of the teacher as a host who welcomes and provides hospitality for students as honored guests. He writes:

> The hospitality metaphor suggests that teachers should develop a situation where children are seen as gifted, honored guests who have something to share with others. They move from controlling students to strategies that provide students with the space to develop their gifts and pursue their calling. . . . Students will seldom believe they have anything to bring unless there is someone who will show their willingness to "receive" them. Indeed, we discover our gifts in the eyes of the receiver. Teachers who can detach themselves from their need to impress and control and who can allow themselves to become recipients will find that it is when the gift is received it becomes more conspicuous.[7]

6. A very helpful recent book on this topic is *Metaphors We Teach By: How Metaphors Shape What We Do in Classrooms*, edited by Ken Badley and Harro Van Brummelen.

7. Makhado and Spalding, "Community and Hospitality in Multicultural Classrooms," 136–37.

Parker Palmer in *The Courage to Teach* records that the metaphor that has shaped his teaching for more than twenty years is that of a sheepdog, one of "the all-business Border collies one sees working the flocks in sheep country." He continues:

> The sheepdog has four vital functions. It maintains a space where the sheep can graze and feed themselves; it holds the sheep together in that space, constantly bringing back strays; it protects the boundaries of the space to keep dangerous predators out; and, when the grazing ground is depleted, it moves with the sheep to another space where they can find the food they need.[8]

Palmer says that a metaphor such as this one can both reveal strengths in us and also suggest shadows in us, e.g., a tendency to regard our students as "sheep" in the negative sense of mindless followers.

The same is true of my personal favorite, which also involves care of sheep—that of the shepherd. I believe that the Lord, the Good Shepherd, calls us to be shepherds to those whom we teach but only if we avoid the "heavy shepherding" of some church leaders who treat their church members as being mindless and make them wholly dependent upon them as leaders. Instead we should seek to be good shepherds who truly care for the sheep.

This involves recognizing and dealing with our students as their individual wants arise—and this means we have to get to know them (and they have to get to know us). Jesus said, "I am the good shepherd; I know my sheep and my sheep know me" (John 10:14). It involves listening—and listening, real listening, is one of the most difficult things to do because it involves a death of the self. We need to discuss with pupils what they perceive, hear, and see in their world. We need to start where they are—as Jesus did in his teaching—in order to take them to where they need to go. Guidance is central to our role as teachers, always humbly acknowledging that we too are learners and always knowing and showing that we have so much more to learn.

8. Palmer, *Courage to Teach*, 148.

The shepherd loves his sheep, and love is the greatest thing in all the world. Love is affirmative. It honors deeply the giftedness of each person and seeks the best in an unoppressive way.

Gardening and Other Metaphors

The teacher-as-gardener metaphor has been very influential in thinking about teaching. It is found in a whole Romanticist tradition that stems from the writings of such as the French philosopher Jean Jacques Rousseau. This is a strongly child-centered movement in which what matters is that the child be allowed to develop naturally, undamaged by harmful influences from the adult world. Rousseau wrote about the ideal education of a boy named Emile, which involved immersing him in the world of nature and enabling him to develop for himself. The metaphor of teaching as gardening is used readily in relation to such a view. The idea of the garden here is that of a natural haven in the midst of a manmade concrete jungle.

However, what seems on the surface to be the same metaphor can have very different roots. In the seventeenth century, long before Rousseau wrote *Emile*, there lived in Europe a Moravian Christian educationalist named Jan Amos Komensky, or John Amos Comenius. Comenius wrote explicitly about teaching as gardening. However, despite similarities between Comenius and Rousseau, there are significant differences, which place Comenius in an educational tradition deeply influenced by Jewish and Christian thought.

Comenius has an understanding of nature that is quite different from that of Rousseau. Nature, for Comenius, is the creation of God, originally good, but corrupted by the fall and restored through God's redemptive activity. In God's redeeming and transforming work the processes of education play a part. We should not therefore leave natural processes to proceed on their own but rather we should actively intervene to discipline and train. He writes:

[A] wild tree will not bring forth sweet fruits until it be planted, watered and pruned by a skilled gardener, so does a man grow of his own accord into a human semblance (just as any brute resembles others of his own class), but is unable to develop into a rational, wise, virtuous and pious creature, unless virtue and piety are first engrafted into him. . . . this must first take place while the plants are young.[9]

Comenius derives the metaphor of the garden directly from the Bible, in particular from the Genesis account of the Garden of Eden. His use of the garden metaphor is also based in his experience of the gardens of his day. The garden was an island of culture in the sea of nature, a place where disciplined beauty was brought forth from the unruliness of nature. It was not, as a progressive educationist or a modern city-dweller might see it, a small intrusion of nature in the territory of human culture and building.

The metaphor of gardening, like that of shepherding, is an image that is present in the Bible and both have immediate and direct relevance to classroom practice. Both point us to the need for the lovingly administered discipline that a good gardener or shepherd gives and away from a laissez-faire permissiveness of the extremes of child-centeredness.

Another image taken from the Bible is used by David Smith and Barbara Carvill in their book *The Gift of the Stranger*. They propose that we see the teaching and learning of a foreign language as a way of loving the stranger. This is deeply rooted in the Bible—from the Levitical instruction to love the stranger as we love ourselves to the story of the Good Samaritan in Luke's Gospel. Seeing teaching in this way enables the teacher of a foreign language to move from a consumerist orientation that focuses on what we can derive from knowledge of another language and visits to another country to a more central interest in the life stories and cultures of the people of that country.

Parker Palmer derives a way of seeing human knowing from the Bible. He points out that in the Western world we tend to see

9. Comenius, *Great Didactic*, 7:1.

knowing as a form of control or mastery. The world is out there and we have to get control over it. We are spectators, detached from the things we are to know. We treat the world as an object to be dissected and manipulated. Our way of knowing is a way that is intended to give us power over the world. In contrast with this view, the Bible speaks of knowing in relational terms. Knowing involves the whole person, heart as well as mind. This is a knowledge that has its source in compassion or love, rather than in the desire to control. Palmer says that "the goal of a knowledge arising from love is the reunification and reconstruction of broken selves and worlds. . . . This love is not a soft and sentimental virtue, not a fuzzy feeling of romance."[10]

These and other metaphors set up interactions between biblical images and educational practices. As we inhabit the world of the Bible and are drawn into its clusters of metaphors and images, links are formed between the Bible and the wholeness of our lives and the practice of our teaching.

These metaphors transform how we think about what we are doing and how we do it. The way we see ourselves in the classroom makes a real difference how we teach—whether as a tough army sergeant or as a loving and caring shepherd, whether as a ringmaster in a circus controlling dangerous animals or as a fellow traveller with our students exploring together the wonders of God's world.

Part of the contribution we can make as Christians is to use more biblical metaphors in discussions of education. We should welcome talk of "vision," "mission," and "service" and we should work against pictures that dehumanize the process, such as pictures taken from the world of the marketplace or manufacturing industry.

10. Palmer, *To Know as We are Known*, 8.

1. As you think of yourself when you are teaching at your best, what are you like?

2. What were the metaphors that seemed to guide your teachers in school? At college or university?

3. What are some of the common and emerging metaphors in educational circles today? In your school? Are they generative . . . or degenerative?

4. How might we respond to the increasing influence of the marketing metaphors in educational contexts? How might it affect the content of our lessons or the approaches that we use? How do these metaphors resonate with those the Bible uses?

5. How can we become more shaped by metaphors that come from the Bible or fit well with a biblical view of people and life?

6. What might the centrality in Scripture of the hospitality metaphor mean for the way we organize classrooms, how we arrange the furniture, or what we put on the walls? What about the students and our relationships with them, and theirs with one another? What might it mean for particular subjects, e.g., the teaching of second or foreign languages?

6

Biblical Models for Our Teaching

IN OUR STUDY OF the varied ways in which, like the inhabitants of a Pacific island, we are shaped by an environment—that of the Bible—we looked first at the shaping effect of our living in the Big Story that the Bible tells us, and we have just now followed this by considering how deeply metaphors influence our thinking and practice and the role of biblical metaphors in particular.

We turn now to how we can be shaped by the models of teaching that we find in the Bible. As a small boy, I wanted to grow up to be like the heroes of the cowboy and adventure stories that I read. As a teenager, I wanted to be like my rugby-playing heroes. I did *not* want to be like my father, but this changed radically when I moved into my twenties and discovered a fresh respect within me for him as a person whose example had deeply influenced and shaped me. How clearly also I now see the ways in which our two grandsons are like their parents, not just in physical appearance but also in little mannerisms and expressions. It is also apparent that the younger of them, who is only two, strives to be like his brother who is five years older. The lives and practices of those who are near to us undoubtedly shape us as people and what we do, both unconsciously and insofar as we consciously seek to be like them and follow their examples. Models have a profound shaping effect upon us as people.

So what of biblical models for education and teaching? Well, although there were no schools in Bible times like our twenty-first-century schools, there were certainly many examples of teachers and learners. Outstanding among them is, of course, Jesus the Teacher, who was addressed as Rabbi or Teacher more than fifty times in the Gospel accounts, and who was also a Learner of whom it was said that as a child he "grew in wisdom" (Luke 2:52) and that as an adult he "learned obedience" (Heb 5:8).

Jesus the Teacher

Biblical models such as that of Jesus the Teacher can shape our educational ministry, not simply by copying in slavish ways or by abstracting principles from what and how he taught that we apply in exactly the same way, but by being shaped by exposure to his example and acting in the spirit of what he did.

I expect that many readers of this book will, at some time or other, have looked at the approaches of Jesus to his work as a teacher. You have probably come up with quite a list of things that characterized Jesus as a teacher. How many of the following would you have listed?

Firstly, Jesus' teaching was *rooted in everyday life*, in the lifeworld of those he was teaching, in their everyday experiences, referring to and pointing to everyday objects and events like lamps and weddings. He told stories, not only to children but also to adults, and they were everyday life stories about mustard seeds, fig trees, vineyards, wedding feasts, and shepherds looking for a lost sheep. He lived out what he taught—perhaps seen supremely in his washing of the disciples' feet—so not only was his teaching presented in everyday life contexts, it was lived in everyday life.

Secondly, Jesus' teaching was *appropriate* for those he was seeking to teach and therefore different for Nicodemus, the woman at the well, the young lawyer, the Sadducees, etc. He began where people were, with the issues that concerned them and the questions that they asked.

Thirdly, Jesus' teaching *provoked thought.* He was concerned to get people to think, not simply to give them answers but to get them to work out the answers for themselves. He drew them on, puzzling them with parables so as to sort out those who would want to go a bit further from those who would not. He used simple language but with layers of meaning. "Whoever takes the lowly position of this child is the greatest in the kingdom of heaven" (Matt 18:4). The words are simple and easy to understand but the meaning is something you can think about and go on thinking about, ever discovering deeper depths. As every good teacher does, Jesus constantly asked leading questions to get people thinking along with him instead of confronting him head-on. The Cambridge theologian Derek Kidner commented on this by saying, "That way, the truth can work its roots down deep into the mind."[1]

Fourthly, Jesus' teaching was *memorable.* There is no denying this! He used short sentences, rhythm, repetition, vivid imagery producing pictures in the mind, humor, overstatement, and riddles. Kidner writes:

> Jesus often took a special delight in putting a thing with wit and zest. Think of that engaging rogue, the unjust steward, managing not only to outsmart his employer but to get the man's customers and tenants nicely compromised as well (and unable to say No whenever he might turn up for a little hospitality later on). Or that battleaxe of a widow who reduces Judge Jefferies' ancestor to a jelly. Or again those wild exaggerations (too familiar to us now) like the man who has a camel in his cup but only notices the fly; or the idiot who would tempt the pigs with a pearl necklace. And there is that teasing mockery about the prophets who are so conveniently dead. "You're the old firm, aren't you! Your fathers did the killing, you put up the monuments."[2]

---

1. Kidner, "Jesus the Teacher." I found this short article by Derek Kidner very helpful indeed when first thinking about Jesus as teacher, and many of the things I am including here were stimulated by reading what he said.

2. Kidner, "Jesus the Teacher," 11.

Fifthly and finally, how inescapable is the fact that Jesus' teaching was *motivated by love*! We see him appealing to the whole person and not just the mind, not putting down his hearers unless their attitude really called for it, authoritative without being authoritarian (a balance not easily maintained by the teacher), and rooted in thorough preparation (which seemed to be more of himself as a person than of the content of his teaching!).

Having said all this, we should not ignore the fact that Jesus was and is unique. Not only is he not a modern classroom teacher but, as the Son of God, he is exercising a degree and kind of authority that none of us can ever exercise. As C. S. Lewis puts it in *Mere Christianity*,

> A man who was merely a man and said the sorts of things Jesus said would not be a great moral teacher: He would either be a lunatic . . . or . . . the devil. . . . You must make your choice. Either this man was, and is, the son of God: or else a madman. . . . [L]et us not come with any . . . nonsense about His being a great human teacher. He has not left that open to us."[3]

We should also bear in mind that it is possible for us to read back into the Gospel accounts what we regard in our contemporary context as good teaching approaches, seeing more than what is actually there and missing things that may be there.

Nevertheless, it does seem very plausible to suggest that there are many things for us to learn from the example of Jesus as teacher, he who said "learn from me" (Matt 11:29), and perhaps not least from the gentleness and humility he mentions in the context of that saying.

Three Modes of Teaching in the Old Testament

I now want to turn to look at Jesus as teacher in what is probably a less familiar way: looking at him through the lens of the Old Testament and, in particular, in the light of three modes of education

3. Lewis, *Mere Christianity*, 52.

that Walter Brueggemann, in his book *The Creative Word*, identifies as corresponding to the three main divisions of the Old Testament: Torah, Prophets, and Writings. In other words, models for teaching can be found in the very shape of the Old Testament.

We look first at the *Torah* and at a key passage, Deuteronomy 6, where Moses utters the *Shema*, that most important of Jewish prayers. We read in verses 4 and 5, "Hear, Israel: The Lord our God, the Lord is one. Love the Lord your God with all your heart and with all your soul and with all your strength." Then, further down, in verse 20, we read, "In the future, when your son asks you, 'What is the meaning of the stipulations . . .'"

The child asks, "What is the meaning?" and the answer is not a logical exposition of a doctrine but the story of God and Israel. What are you to do when a child asks for meaning? Tell him a story, tell him the story that teaches him who he is and who his people are, where he has come from, where he is going, where he belongs.

Teaching in the Torah mode is teaching that gives us identity, teaching that tells us who we are and where we are and provides security in all the unexpected events that happen to us. We think of Torah as Law, as Ten Commandments, as a burning mountain, but the heart of the message of the early books of the Bible is that it sets out an orderly, trustworthy lifeworld in which the child can feel safe, in which you and I and the children that we teach can feel safe, safe in the care of the Lord our God who was and who is and who always will be.

We turn, secondly, to the *Prophets* and, in particular, to the book of the prophet-shepherd Amos, as he proclaims to Israel, "The lion has roared—who will not fear?" (Amos 3:8). He speaks not of a mighty beast that he has heard in the thicket, where it prowled seeking animal or even human prey. This lion is the Sovereign Lord! "The Sovereign Lord has spoken—who can but prophesy?" After dealing with the nations round about them and with their southern cousins in Judah, Amos turns his fire on Israel and he tells them that the Lord hates their songs and worship because they deny justice to the poor and trample upon them. He continues, "Woe to you who are complacent in Zion and to you who feel secure on Mount Samaria" (Amos 6:1).

The problem was that the people had the Law, the Torah, and they had settled down. They were satisfied that they had got it right. They thought they knew everything that was important. They had nothing more to learn. Children and young people can become like that, their curiosity and urge to find out new things all gone. The most difficult students to teach are not the badly behaved—they can be challenging and even fun to teach! The most difficult are the ones who think they have nothing to learn! People in our churches can be like that. They come not to learn . . . but to check out the soundness of the preaching! You and I can be like that.

We rarely question how we look at life in the world. We rarely question the prevailing views in our culture or in our church sub-culture. We need prophetic teaching that shakes us up, that leads us to ask the big questions, to look at things in a new way.

Our teaching, in turn, should be not only passing on the truth, telling students who they are, and making them secure in their identity, but also shaking them up, challenging them to think anew, to see things in a new and different way, and to question what they and everybody else around them seem to believe. We need to help them to both firm commitment and an openness to learn and gain new insights and this is not an easy balance to attain or maintain.

The Old Testament contains the Law and the Prophets but there is also a third section, and this corresponds to Brueggemann's third mode. This is the mode of *Wisdom* in the Writings, books like Psalms and the Wisdom literature of Job, Proverbs, and Ecclesiastes, and also the Song of Songs and the stories of Ruth and Esther, Ezra and Nehemiah, Daniel and the Lamentations of Jeremiah. The third kind of Old Testament teacher is the teacher of wisdom, the one who teaches us how we are to live together in God's world, how to promote justice in society and combat injustice.

This is not the spectator knowledge of the person watching the football game, not the theoretical knowledge that we can talk and talk about; it is the on-the-playing-field knowledge of what we are to do. Knowing *how* to do and say things and *when* to do and say them.

Some of our students know all about the theories of science and the study of literature, earn the best grades, and receive the most prestigious diplomas, but they don't know how to live, how to relate to other people, how to apply their knowledge wisely and justly, or how to make decisions about what to do next! What do children and teenagers want to know? They want to know how to make and keep friends! And some of the most knowledgeable in a factual sense may be the least wise and the worst at forming relationships!

Jesus the Torah Teacher, the Prophetic Teacher, and the Wisdom Teacher

Jesus is the Great Teacher, the model teacher, and in him we find the three kinds of teacher of the Old Testament: the Torah teacher who teaches us who we are, the prophetic teacher who teaches us to think and ask questions, and the teacher of wisdom who teaches us to live wisely and justly in the world with other people.

Jesus is a Torah teacher, a teacher of the Law. Hear him in the Sermon on the Mount in Matthew 5–7. Over and over and over again, he says "your Father in Heaven" or "your heavenly Father" or "your Father," and right at the heart of it he says that they should pray like this: "Our Father in heaven . . ." Altogether no fewer than sixteen times Jesus talks about God as Father—his Father, their Father, our Father! You are worried? Don't worry, for your Father knows what you need. There as Jesus teaches them the Law of God, what they should do to please God, the heart of it is telling them who they are, that they have a Father who cares.

Jesus is also the prophetic teacher. He said he had come to fulfill the law but he asked people questions about their understanding. Are you really living the way God wants you to live?

"You have heard that it was said, 'Love your neighbor and hate your enemy.' But I tell you, love your enemies . . . that you may be children of your Father in heaven'" (Matt 5:43–45). Jesus taught them to ask questions and he did this, as every good teacher does, by asking questions himself—lots and lots of questions—and by saying things to get them to think, things that shocked them.

Jesus is also the wisdom teacher. As we saw earlier, he taught in parables and riddles, with proverbs and wise sayings. The language is simple but the thought is deep. He talks about wise men building houses on a rock, camels and eyes of a needle, and taking out the log that is in one's own eye rather than the speck that is in another's eye. So much of it could come straight from the book of Proverbs, and it is all about how to live in the world and with one another, within the home, and with your neighbors and colleagues. It is all about wisdom and discernment, justice and fairness.

We need all three modes in our schools and churches. If we only teach people what to believe, we make them secure but self-satisfied, or we turn them off and alienate them. If we only teach them to ask questions, then they never know what to believe—always questions and never answers, no security. If we only teach them practical life lessons, they never get to see the big picture of God's world and never explore beyond the limits of their present knowledge.

It is like using a three-legged milking stool. My father was a farmer who milked cows by hand when I was a boy. He would take a stool and sit by the cow with his head against its side. The stool had three legs. If it had only one leg, he could not have sat on it at all. If it had two legs, he could perhaps have supported himself on it with his head against the cow's side but it would have been very unstable. It had three legs and all three legs were needed.

We need Torah teachers, prophetic teachers, and wisdom teachers in our schools and in our churches. May we follow Jesus in being, as far as we can and between ourselves and our colleagues, all three for those we teach, those with whom we seek to communicate.

1. Think about which kind of teachers you had as a young person, which kind you are, and which kinds of teachers your colleagues are (Torah or prophetic or a teacher of wisdom).

2. Is it possible for each teacher to strive for a balance of the three teaching modes? Are there ways in which you and they could be complementary in your roles within your school or department? How can you avoid the potential for confusion among students and instead speak with one voice?

3. Is or should the balance between modes be different with children and young people of different ages? Are all the modes relevant at all ages?

7

Biblical Principles for Our Teaching

WE HAVE BEEN THINKING together about how the Bible influences and shapes us in our whole lives and in our work as teachers. The Bible is like an environment, e.g., that of a Pacific island, in which we live and by which we are shaped. We have looked at the shaping influence of the biblical story and stories, of biblical metaphors, and of biblical models, but so far little has been said about biblical statements and it is to this very important aspect that we now turn.

The Bible Says . . .

With the oil lamp flickering beside me, I would sit and twiddle the knobs on the radio, searching amid the crackles and whistles of the static, trying to tune in to Radio Luxembourg. This was in the 1950s and we didn't call it a radio then—it was a "wireless."

Radio Luxembourg was very popular with teenagers like me across Western Europe because it was the only radio station broadcasting pop music at the time. By the way, the word "teenager" had come over from America at about that time, so we were Europe's first teenagers! And then, as now, teenagers and popular music went together and, in spite of my father's impatient requests that

I lower the volume of "that noise," I was, in that respect at least, a typical teenager of the times.

However, although I enjoyed those music programs, I was also very impressed by a rather different program that came from the same radio station, a program called *The Hour of Decision*. I would listen every week—I think it was on Wednesdays from 7:00 to 7:30 p.m.—to half an hour of hearty singing of hymns and songs and a sermon by the evangelist Billy Graham. I liked these programs because they provided a change from the more formal and traditional church life that I was growing up with in rural Ireland at that time.

Over and over again as he preached, Billy Graham would proclaim with emphasis, "The Bible says . . ." Quite often, as I remember, he would complete the sentence with the words ". . . you must be born again" but there were many other things too that he recounted as being things that the Bible says. I had grown up with the Bible. It had a very important place in our lives as a family but somehow its relevance to me personally was not something I was clearly aware of. But here was a man who was saying with conviction that it is relevant to *me*, it has things to say to *me*. It is not just that "The Bible *said* . . ." but that "The Bible *says* . . ." The Bible speaks today and it speaks to people like you and me! It has things to say to us that are of central importance! I was excited at this thought fifty years ago and I am still excited by it today. This unique book contains statements the ultimate source of which is God, statements that are important to me in my everyday life, in my work as well as my worship. I derive life principles from what the Bible says to me.

Biblical Principles for the Classroom

Biblical principles for life . . . and for schools and classroom teaching? Among those that are commonly suggested for education are such as:

- Education should lead to a better knowledge of God.
- Parents are ultimately responsible before God for the nurture and training of their children.
- Education should prepare people for service to God rather than self-advancement.
- Children should be educated in accord with their God-given nature.

Some of these principles come fairly directly from the Bible, e.g., the principle of parental responsibility. Others are deduced from other things the Bible says, e.g., we are created by God, therefore we should educate children according to how God has made them.

Solidly based biblical principles are essential to our thinking about education but we do well to recognize also that they are in their very nature general, and because they are they do not on their own lead decisively to particular lines of action in particular situations at particular times. The principle of parental responsibility for the education of their children—one that I expect that most of us would put near the top of our list—does not in itself tell us whether we should educate our children at home or in schools and, if the latter, what kind of school we should choose for them.

Again, a school might have as a principle that we should love and affirm each child as being made in the image of God. This sounds like a very good biblical principle. I would be very happy if it were a principle in any school in which I was a teacher or in which my grandchildren were students! It tells us about the attitudes we should have to the children that we teach, but it does not tell us exactly what we should do, for example, about testing and grading!

In the UK in recent years, and I think in many other countries as well, children have been given many more tests than they used to be. What has been happening as a result is that teachers are learning to teach to the test so that their schools come high up in the published tables of school performance. It could be argued that this is not real teaching, that students are not being loved and affirmed, or that some are being loved and affirmed more than others. As a young person, I was always very good at tests and examinations but some students, because of their temperaments, never do well in tests and always fail to do justice to their abilities and knowledge.

On the other hand, it could be argued that, on the basis of the same principle of love, we should test and grade because our students need the examination results and certificates to be able to fit into our society as it is (with its emphasis on testing) and to do well in it. Therefore, it could be concluded, testing and grading is the loving thing to do.

I am *not* saying which argument is right. My point is that the principle on its own does not tell us exactly what to do. The Bible does not tell us exactly what to do in each and every classroom situation but I fear that we sometimes want the Bible to be more than it is.

Does it follow from this that a principles-based approach to teaching and learning is of no use and should be abandoned? God forbid! Some have argued that the Bible has no relevance to education for the very reason that its principles are general, but that is a mistake as great as saying that because moral principles are general we have no need of them!

We do need to have biblical principles for education but we also need to take into account in our planning and decision-making issues to do with national history and culture, age and stage of development of students, gender, race, experience and capabilities of teachers, availability of resource materials, socio-economic factors, and many more.

The same is true of living in the Bible's story or being shaped by its metaphors or models. None of them on their own tell us exactly what to do. All the ways in which the Bible shapes us require interpretation and application. We have to work out as God is working within us!

Functions of Biblical Principles

We also need to be aware of the different ways in which biblical principles function in our thinking about classroom practices.

Biblical principles can be taken to *exclude* some practices, e.g., teaching students to engage in astrology (which would be permitted in a Hindu school) or viewing pornography on the classroom computer.

There are also many practices about which biblical principles are *neutral*; they neither exclude them nor permit them. One example would be using technology in the classroom (although there are some Christians, e.g., the Amish people in the US or the Exclusive Brethren in many countries, who might not approve of using modern computers and other technology). Another example would be the way we arrange the desks in the classroom (our country's laws may require certain kinds of arrangement but biblical principles would not). Other examples would include teaching chess or asking students to work in pairs.

The Bible *commends* certain practices. For example, the Bible urges us to think about what is true and beautiful but it doesn't require us to look at a particular website or read a particular book. It requires us to care for our bodies but it doesn't tell us whether we should teach football or athletics as we help our students to care for their bodies.

Principles apply to the attitudes of our hearts as well as to our actions. Biblical principles tell us that we should have attitudes of love, humility, hospitality, and many more. As recorded in Matthew 18, Jesus urges us to be humble like little children and to welcome little children in his name. There are lots of different actions that would express humility and hospitality—we can choose the actions but we have no choice about *being* humble and welcoming, for these attitudes are always required of us as followers of Jesus.

At the same time, biblical principles condemn other attitudes. Again, in Matthew 18 Jesus says we are not to look down on any of these little ones that we teach. They are not mere "kids" to be patronized; they are human beings like us, persons like us, and they respond to being listened to and talked with as such!

Let's monitor ourselves or ask a colleague to monitor us for the language and tone of how we talk with individual students that we teach or how we address the whole class or school. Do we speak to them from above or talk with them as people?

1. What are some implications of viewing children as being made in the image of God? What might it mean for the methods and approaches that we use in the classroom?

2. How well does the biblical principle of hospitality to the marginalized fit with your school policy or your own attitude on admittance and exclusion?

3. Take justice or fairness or another biblical principle that you might apply to your work in the classroom. Consider a school or classroom issue to which it could apply and see what other considerations would enter your thinking in coming to a decision on that issue.

8

The Bible and the
Content of Our Teaching

WE SAW IN THE last chapter that the Bible shapes us and our classroom practices through the principles that we derive or deduce from what it says, principles that we apply to what we do and how we teach. Another way in which statements in the Bible may shape our classroom teaching is through the impact of what it says upon the *content* of our lessons. This is more specifically about what we take God to be saying to be the case with him and his world and what these things mean for the content of what we teach in the classroom in the different subjects of the school curriculum.

If the Bible or, more broadly, religious studies is a subject in our school curriculum, then the Bible will form part of the content of lessons in that subject. Situations vary greatly across the world and, although the Bible may be totally excluded from the school curriculum in some countries, there are many in which it is acceptable and even expected that it should be included in this way.

But what of the teaching of other subjects in the curriculum? Does the Bible have relevance to the content of our teaching in subjects as diverse as mathematics, science, art, music, history, geography, and all the other subjects that make up the written curriculum? This brings us into what some contemporary Christian writers on education describe as "biblical integration." It is not the main focus of this little book. Many others have written extensively and thoughtfully on this and I am not sure that I can add much to what they have said. Nevertheless, it is an important aspect of our work in the classroom so I will pass on some ideas that I have found helpful.

Opening Windows on God's World

I suggest that we should think of ourselves as not simply teaching subjects in school, but rather as opening windows on God's world and helping our students to focus on the world through them.

Each window shows a different aspect. Through one window we see the world in terms of shapes and numbers; we see the world mathematically. Through another window we see the world historically; we see it in terms of the sequence of events in space and time. Through another window we see it psychologically, or biologically or chemically or morally or linguistically, and so on.

For example, think about an object in the world, a ring.[1] Think about its *mathematical* aspects, what mathematical shape or shapes we see, what its dimensions are. This is looking at the ring through the mathematical window.

Then think about its *physical* aspect through the world of the science of physics. Look at it in terms of the atoms of which it is composed and how they interact. Look at it in terms of its *chemical* components, the elements that combine in the molecules of which it is made.

We can also think about the *history* of rings and the *cultural* customs that surround the wearing of rings, for example, wedding rings. Why do we wear rings, on which fingers? How have the customs changed and developed through time and how do they differ from one culture to another?

1. This example is borrowed from Peck and Strohmer, *Uncommon Sense*, 147–48.

We can also think about the *artistic* aspects of the ring, the beauty of its design and shape, or the work of the craftsperson who made it.

A jeweler will be interested in an *economic* perspective on the ring. How much is it worth? How much can he get for selling it? He may look at my ring and offer me some money for it but I may say that it is worth far more to me. This is the ring that symbolizes my marriage to the woman that I love. We exchanged rings when we were married so this ring has *legal* and *moral* significance to me.

More than that, as a Christian, it is for me linked to the day when my wife and I promised before God to love another as long as we live, so it has *theological* significance for me too.

Seeing the Whole Picture

These perspectives are distinct but, at the same time, all of them are related together as parts of a whole picture of God's world. We should therefore be looking for ways in which we can help students to develop a whole perspective, to synthesize as well as analyze.

We may do this by team teaching, which looks at the same time at different aspects of a theme, e.g., a cross-curricular study focused on Egypt looking at its biology, history, and mathematics.

Alternatively, as individual teachers of particular subjects, we may look for opportunities to bring in other aspects into the teaching of our main subject, e.g., bringing history and personal faith into mathematics or science by telling something of the life stories of famous people in those areas and their motivations—say, the way that Georg Cantor's Christian faith and his desire to understand the idea of eternity motivated his massive study of infinity and development of the theory of mathematical sets.

This means that what is often called "biblical integration"[2] is, in part, the setting of what we are teaching in our subject area

2. I personally prefer not to use this term because it can so easily be taken to suggest that the Bible is being added to neutral, objective subject matter, when in fact all subject matter reflects God's design, is affected by sin, and is redeemed in Christ. This is why I prefer to talk in terms of locating our

into the larger context of a fuller and wider perspective on life in God's world. Or, putting it another way, we are locating our teaching of our subject in the Big Story of God, the story of creation, fall, redemption, and the new world to come.

Integration and Pseudo-integration

I have found very helpful the way Harold Klassen, a Christian educator from Canada who travels widely across the world, puts this kind of approach in his account of what he calls the "Visual Valet." As Harold puts it,

> The natural inclination, when trying to integrate the Bible with other subjects taught in school, is to add the Bible to the subject. However, Biblical integration lies in the opposite direction. The subjects being taught need to find their place in the "big picture" of what God has done and is doing in His creation. Without a clear framework to understand the "big picture," it is difficult to relate anything to it and impossible to clearly communicate the relationships to anyone else.[3]

I have seen many examples of integration that is poorly done, what could be termed "pseudo-integration." The Bible is added to the subject in a way that is artificial or contrived. Quotations from the Bible may be connected to the topic being studied by mere word association or spiritualization.

Here is an example from a textbook:

> In this chapter we have studied relations. In mathematics, relations are sets of ordered pairs. In general, people are related when they are connected by marriage or ancestry. Spiritually, every Christian is related to Jesus Christ and God the Father (Gal 4:1–7 & 1 John 4:14–16) as well as to all other Christians (Eph 2:19).[4]

---

teaching of the subject in the Big Story of God.

3. Klassen, "Visual Valet."

4. Pilger and Tagliapietra, *Algebra 1*, 268.

Another example is of the addition of the biblical mandate to "be fruitful and multiply" to a page of mathematical multiplication tasks to be completed by the student.

Here the Bible texts do not genuinely address the mathematical topic at hand; they are there as a kind of holy decoration. Indeed, they tend to lower the status of the topic being studied and make it a human secular activity that has to be somehow made holy or spiritual by the addition of largely irrelevant Bible verses. The mathematical task is no longer a matter of looking through the mathematical window at God's wonderful world; it has become something mundane in need of hallowing by the addition of a quotation from the Bible.

A good test is whether your approach is from the inside out or from the outside in! If you are coming into your subject from the outside and bringing the Bible in from the outside, then what you are doing is probably artificial and contrived. You are not doing science or mathematics or psychology or whatever, you are spiritualizing it! On the other hand, if what you are doing is, say, genuinely and integrally mathematical (or scientific or geographical or linguistic or whatever), and you or your students find it pointing outwards to God and the Bible, that is a different matter. For example, if you are studying fractals and you conclude, as some have done, that the Mandelbrot Fractal is worthy of being termed "the thumbprint of God,"[5] that is not spiritualizing or Christianizing mathematics: it is bringing into the foreground what is there within the subject. It is opening and looking through a window on God's world and discovering that it is indeed God's world!

This setting of what we are teaching in the wider context of God's world and the multiple perspectives we can take on it may also lead us to take particular approaches within our subject area. For example, in teaching psychology, we are likely to favor more personalist approaches over, say, a behaviorist approach that reduces the human being to his or her outward behavior. Our view of history

5. Fractal geometry shows how relatively simple mathematical formulae can be used with the aid of modern high-speed computers to generate beautiful shapes found everywhere in nature.

will not be the cyclical one of Eastern religion. We may see mathematics as more a matter of discovery than of human creation.

Studying the Bible Itself

Another way in which the Bible may be related to the content of our teaching is in it itself being studied from within a subject area. For example, we can use the Bible as content in the study and teaching of literature. Leland Ryken writes:

> There is a quiet revolution going on in the study of the Bible. At its center is a growing awareness that the Bible is a work of literature and that the methods of literary scholarship are a necessary part of any complete study of the Bible.[6]

In a *Time* magazine article, David Van Biema writes:

> The Bible is the most influential book ever written . . . the best-selling book of all time. . . . In a 1992 survey of English teachers to determine the top-10 required books for high school English classes, plays by Shakespeare occupied three spots and the Bible none. And yet . . . according to one estimate, Shakespeare alludes to Scripture some 1,300 times.[7]

Can we understand works of English literature like Shakespeare's plays without knowledge of the Bible? And is this not also true of literature in other languages? Again, Van Biema says, "The Bible is the most influential book ever written . . . " so can we understand history without a knowledge of the Bible?

As linguists, we might study the grammar of Old Testament Hebrew or New Testament Greek. As psychologists we might study the heights and depths of human experience expressed in the Psalms or as philosophers the views of meaning and purpose found in Ecclesiastes. As mathematicians, we might study the mathematics of the Bible.

6. Ryken, *How to Read the Bible as Literature*, 11.
7. Van Biema, "Case for Teaching the Bible."

Possible Misuses of the Bible

In studying the Bible from within a subject area, I suggest that we need to be aware of the possibilities of misuse of what we believe to be the authoritative word of God.

For example, in looking at the mathematics of the Bible, we may note its rounding of numbers, e.g., in its recording that five thousand were fed by Jesus and his disciples, or the approximation of π (3.14159 . . .) to three in 1 Kings 7:23, where a circular object in Solomon's temple is stated to have a diameter of ten cubits and a circumference of thirty cubits. We might even note a curious example where a number in the Bible is not rounded (the catch of 153 fish recorded in John 21) and speculate whether it is significant that this is one of Pascal's triangular numbers. Such speculation can lead quickly into the mystical realms of numerology, and to use the Bible in this way seems somewhat removed from a rightful use of the word of God.

I have similar concerns about such practices as the use of Bible passages to teach English grammar. Asking students to underline the nouns or the verbs in a passage from the Bible is also, I would suggest, possible misuse of the authoritative word of God. God did not give us the Bible for it to be reduced to a mere tool for teaching something that could just as well be taught using other materials. Indeed, is there not more than a hint of manipulation and indoctrination in such practices?! Biblical truths are not being studied as such; instead, they are being implanted while the attention of the student is focussed elsewhere!

Although it may sound like hyperbole to say so, is this practice not similar to one allegedly used in education in Afghanistan in the 1980s when resistance fighters were being recruited to fight against the Russians and, it is said, a third-grade mathematics textbook asked, "One group of mujahedeen attack 50 Russian soldiers. In that attack 20 Russians are killed. How many Russians fled?" Again, it is said, a fourth-grade textbook contained this question: "The speed of a Kalashnikov bullet is 800 meters per second. If a Russian is at a distance of 3200 meters from a mujahidin, and that mujahidin aims at the Russian's head, calculate how many seconds it will take for the bullet to strike the Russian in the forehead." I have to add that I have no way of checking the truth of these accounts, which can be found, like much that is not true, on the Internet.

This may be a very extreme and not very subtle example but the point is that we would generally view such a practice, whether or not it ever actually happened, as being unacceptable manipulation or even brainwashing. It is not only the unworthiness of the aims or the extremeness of the context that makes it unacceptable, it is the fact that the student's attention is focused on the mathematical task and the worldview is being implanted without him noticing it. Much more subtle is the cultural and racial bias that can be found in examples teachers use or in standardized tests.

People can also be manipulated into accepting something that is true and good whilst their attention is on a task, but its truth and goodness does not justify the use of such approaches.

I have mentioned some good examples of how the Bible can be related to the content of what we teach and also a few of what I regard as examples of bad practice. It is my fervent hope that the bad examples will not dissuade you from the great work of opening windows of many kinds on God's wonderful world.

1. Think of some examples of what you might regard as ways in which the Bible can properly relate to the content of a subject that you teach.

2. Think also of any examples of pseudo-integration in your subject area.

3. How would you define the line of demarcation between the two?

9

Living Letters in the Classroom

THE SUBJECT OF THIS little book has been the various interrelated ways in which we as teachers and what we do in our classrooms can be shaped by the Bible, or, more precisely, by God through the Bible. We have been thinking of the Bible as being like an environment in which we live and move, an environment that has multiple aspects all of which have their impact upon us and our teaching.

We are being shaped as *people* who teach. In other words, *we* are being transformed and our teaching is being transformed.

Living Letters from Christ

From my earliest days as a Christian believer, I realized that personal holiness of character was important. As young Christians, we sang a song that had this refrain:

> Be like Jesus, this my song,
> In the home and in the throng,
> Be like Jesus all day long,
> I would be like Jesus.

I was taught that sanctification should be a growing reality within me. I was familiar with the words of Paul in 2 Corinthians where, having described how Moses' face shone after he met with God and pointed out that this was something that gradually faded away, he writes, "And we all, who with unveiled faces contemplate the Lord's glory, are being transformed into his likeness with ever-increasing glory, which comes from the Lord, who is the Spirit" (2 Cor 3:18).

I remember a lady who worked in rural Ireland with a Christian organization called the Faith Mission and how her face would shine when she was talking with us young people about the Lord and his work. In that same chapter from 2 Corinthians, Paul writes that his readers "show that you are a letter from Christ . . . written not with ink but with the Spirit of the living God, not on tablets of stone but on tablets of human hearts" (3:3). If ever there was a living letter from Christ, it seemed to me that this godly lady was one. She was one of my inspirations as I went to work in that insurance office in Dublin. I wanted to be a living letter to be known and read by all my colleagues.

If we have turned to Christ, we are being changed! We are to show his glory in our beings. We are to be the fragrance of Christ. We are to be living letters to be known and read by everybody, including the children and young people that we teach! We are to be the living curriculum for our students.

Those who write and speak about being a Christian in the workplace and in all of life and our relationships with others often refer to this as "incarnation." Because incarnation in the Bible is centrally about God becoming a human being in Jesus rather than about principles and virtues being lived out by us, it is questionable whether it is the best word to use. A better word is, I suggest, "embodiment." The Bible shapes character in particular ways and that is what makes a difference in the classroom or any other workplace. The Bible's message becomes embodied in us as our ways of living are moulded by it. When this does not happen, it is often said that "what we are shouts so loud that people cannot hear what we say." For the teacher this means, in Parker Palmer's pithy and memorable phrase, "we teach who we are."[1]

1. Palmer, *Courage to Teach*, 1.

60

It is Not Always Easy

It is not always easy to show the grace and gentleness of Christ in all classroom situations. The Scottish Reformer Samuel Rutherford wrote that "grace groweth best in winter."[2] For some of us who are called to teach, the school and classroom can at times be a very wintry place (although, at many other times, it can be the greatest place to be in all the world!).

David Smith writes of his first days as a teacher and of what he terms "a bruising encounter" with a text from 2 Timothy that says, "the Lord's servant . . . must be kind to everyone, able to teach, not resentful. Opponents must be gently instructed" (2 Tim 2:24–25). At the same time, he was having another, even more bruising encounter with the students of a local secondary school. He writes:

> In those weeks my first frustrating, fumbling efforts at teaching teenagers tested my ability to remain civil, let alone gentle. Some were unruly, some were discourteous, some were openly keen to test the mettle of the new student teacher. One eleven-year-old stripped to the waist while I was writing on the blackboard, apparently just to see what I would do. Many evenings I returned home exasperated and discouraged. Given the yawning gap between my experience and what I was reading (Kind to *everyone*? *Never* resentful? *Full* of mercy? Even with *that* class?), it did not take long for my reforming zeal to be humbled. Somehow *living* all of these qualities was a whole lot harder than solving intellectual puzzles; in addition to understanding, I needed grace.
>
> I am sure that some of that gap still yawns, but I also trust that my ongoing interaction with those texts has had some impact on the nature of my teaching. It immediately caused me to reflect on some of the teaching I saw around me. A colleague kept his classes in a state of awed submission which made me envious, but appeared to do so in large measure through the use of biting sarcasm when students stepped out of line. They came to fear the lash of his tongue. *Kind* to everyone? Full of *mercy*? These

2. Rutherford, *Loveliness of Christ*, 12.

commanding words may not have told me exactly how to teach, but they did help me not only to realize that there were some character qualities which I needed to work on, but also to decide that there were some models of teaching which I did *not* wish to follow.[3]

David is not alone: many of us can tell of bruising encounters in the classroom, not only with individual students but in struggles against deeply rooted racial, social, cultural, and gender prejudice and injustices of many kinds. We battle with forces that are hostile to our attempts to be like Jesus. Wintry conditions may prevail in our broken world of broken relationships and, if so, there our resources of authentic Christian character are so sorely needed.

Being Nice Is Not Enough

However, it is an (all too) easy step to go from saying something along these lines to the conclusion that what *really* matters is the kind of people that we are, and even that *all* that really matters is the kind of people that we are. We may say that if there is a Christian teacher in the classroom, then God is present in the classroom and this is all that matters. We may say that if a school is staffed by Christian teachers, then this makes it a Christian school.

Against this, I would want to argue that although an emphasis on embodiment is absolutely *necessary* to relating the Bible to what we do in our schools, this emphasis on its own is not *sufficient*. On its own, it becomes too narrowly focussed on the individual Christian and her personal character. Taken on its own, we might think that being a Christian teacher is simply a matter of being a nice, caring, loving, gracious person. But it is more than being nice. We could be nice in the service of a cause that is not good. We could be nice and be the train drivers who took thousands of people to the concentration camps in World War II. We could be nice and work in a factory manufacturing cigarettes, which lead to the painful deaths of many people.

3. Smith and Shortt, *Bible and the Task of Teaching*, 36.

We are told that Francis of Assisi said, "Preach the gospel always and, if necessary, use words." His words highlight how essential it is that we should be living letters, but I sometimes fear that what he says could be taken to mean that we never need to use words in our witness to Christ. Perhaps "Preach the gospel always and, when appropriate, use words" would be a better way to put it (and especially good advice for those of us who use too many words!).

The danger of an exclusive focus on personal character is that Christian teaching may be reduced to being a nice person, with little effort to think through wider educational issues. This can lead to a situation in which prevailing educational practices are accepted uncritically. It is possible to be a nice person whilst teaching with unworthy aims, manipulative approaches, and false content. Developing Christian virtues cannot remain at the level of personal qualities. It has to influence our approaches, methods and content as well as our educational aims, our motivations for teaching, and our thinking about each of these areas.

Teaching and learning are themselves in part moral affairs. In his book *Exiles from Eden*, Mark Schwehn argues, for example, that "some degree of humility is a precondition for learning."[4] Humility is a Christian virtue but it is not always highly rated in other approaches to ethics and it may not be highly rated by our students. Teaching such virtues is not simply a matter of exemplifying them but of taking steps to organize teaching and learning so that they are promoted. If we take seriously the call to be living letters from Christ in the classroom and to follow it through consistently, it may lead to a reshaping of the whole teaching process.

An emphasis on embodiment therefore demands that we also take seriously all the other ways in which the Bible shapes our classroom teaching. If we are to become truly the kind of people we ought to be, then we will also be concerned to take biblical principles seriously, to live in God's story, to indwell the imagery of the Bible and attend to how it resonates or conflicts with the imagery of contemporary culture, and to see that the way we teach

4. Schwehn, *Exiles from Eden*, 49.

is modelled on good examples from the Bible and especially that of Jesus, the Great Teacher. In an often-hostile world, the mode we need may be that of the prophet who unmasks injustice and works for reconciliation.

1. What kind of character do your students see in you?

2. Think of ways in which you could organize classroom learning to promote the development of virtues like humility, hospitality, honesty, and unselfishness.

3. In what practical ways can you set the example for your students in the classroom?

10

Getting It All Together

THROUGH THIS BOOK, WE have been thinking of our being shaped by the Bible (or rather, by God through the Bible) as like being shaped by the varied elements of a new environment, e.g., that of a remote Pacific island.

There is a holism to that shaping. The shaping elements may be distinct but they are interrelated (weather, flora and fauna, food, lifestyles of people, customs and culture, etc.). Similarly, biblical statements, story, metaphors, and models are all part of a whole shaping influence of the Bible upon us.

Shaping by the Bible is holistic in another way too: it is a shaping of the whole person in a process that is both life-long and life-wide. In addition, in the case of a calling as relational as that of teaching, it is in turn concerned with the whole person of every student and their life-long and life-wide learning and development.

All These Ways of Shaping Work Together

In the book that David Smith and I wrote, *The Bible and the Task of Teaching*, we used the image of a multi-stranded rope to describe these links between the Bible and our daily life and work. Just as the strands of the rope overlap and interweave, with no single strand functioning as the core of the rope, so the different ways of relating the Bible to teaching overlap and interweave. We need the whole rope, all the interrelated strands.

So what is being advocated in this book is a holistic approach that brings together all these different elements of the relationship. It seeks to provide for the richness and diversity of all that makes up the Bible—its statements and principles, its narrative form, its rich store of metaphors, and the range of its educational modes and models. (Our exploration in chapter 2 of the metaphors that we use in thinking about what the Bible is and does was intended to bring to light something of this rich diversity of its nature and function.)

We have just seen at the end of chapter 9 how a focus on Christian character quickly takes us to the other ways in which the Bible can be related to our teaching.

Similarly, taking biblical principles seriously should lead us to attend to the big picture, the Big Story of the Bible in which they are embedded and apart from which they are not really meaningful—the imagery with which they are often associated, the models in which they are personified, and the virtues of true Christian character without which, as 1 Corinthians 13:1 puts it, I am only "a resounding gong or a clanging cymbal." An exclusive emphasis on biblical statements can be very legalistic and rationalistic.

An exclusive emphasis on stories and on living in the Big Story of God can become quite situational without statements of principle that provide the boundaries within which we are to live. Living in the story also calls for the metaphors that open up new ways of seeing things and doing things and enhances the creativity of the actors as they seek to live out the missing act 5. And for the Christian teacher, the model teachers who tower over the scenes of acts 1–4 given in the Bible must continually inspire and challenge us as we seek to live and teach in the ongoing drama of God's Big Story.

Metaphors alone, stripped of their context in the Big Story of the Bible and of the requirements of its principles and the examples of its models, can embed contradictory views of human nature and life, as we saw with the contrast between the uses of the gardening metaphor in the writings of Comenius and Rousseau.

Models alone can become unrelated examples pointing in different ways and causing confusion. They need the framework of the Big Story in which to understand and appreciate them and in the context of which also to apply them in our day and time. They need to be lived in that Big Story and embodied in daily life and work.

Shaping Is of the Whole Person

Not only are we being shaped by the whole environment of the Bible, the shaping is also of us as whole persons living and teaching in that environment. The shaping is of the whole person rather than just of one's reasoning processes. It includes them but it is not confined to them. Imagination and creativity also have their place. Emotions too are brought into play as we are drawn into stories, explore the association of clusters of metaphors, and seek to learn from our model teachers. Reason and passion are brought together in the shaping of us as whole persons.

This shaping is not only of us as whole persons, it is for the wholeness of our lives. It is not just for the private and devotional areas of thought and life but also for the whole of life and our work as teachers.

This is, in its turn, a service to whole persons and communities and in communion with others similarly called. This teaching ministry is also for the whole of the lives of those to whom the ministry comes—that is, for example, what teaching in the wisdom mode is about. It is for all the phases and stages of their lives (childhood, teenage, working life, marriage, career, retirement, old age, even preparation for that last great adventure—that of death) and for all the different kinds of activity we engage in (study, making things, employment, sport and leisure, family life and homemaking, and even the forced inactivity of illness or old age). In other words, it is life-long and life-wide.

It is a shaping that transforms us as people and as teachers and therefore transforms all our relationships—with ourselves, with one another, with the world in which God has placed us, and with God himself. This is another respect in which it can be holistic for us and for those we teach and with whom we learn.

The shaping (and being shaped) that is being proposed is, however, not by the Bible in itself; it is by the one who caused it to be written and who speaks to us in and through it. In *The Last Word*, Tom Wright reminds us that the phrase "the authority of Scripture" is, or should be, a shorthand for God's authority exercised through Scripture, "a dynamic force within God's people . . . energizing them for mission . . . and ordering their lives accordingly."[1] The Bible is therefore the "vehicle of the Spirit's authority . . . energizing, shaping and directing the church,"[2] and, we could add, us as we go to teach in the classrooms to which he has called us.

It is a matter of God speaking, of God being active within and among us, but we are not passive robots. We are called to be active, to study, to work, to think and imagine, to question, to love and relate, and so much more, thereby serving God and those to whom we seek to minister in educational contexts. We seek to interpret and apply the Bible in a way that avoids reduction to literalist or rationalist extremes and brings trust and commitment together with openness and questioning.

Having said all this, does it take us beyond vague generalizations which make no real difference in practice? I believe with all my heart that it can and I pray that it will.

1. Wright, *Last Word*, 127.
2. Ibid., 51.

Bibliography

Anderson, Gary A. *Sin: A History*. New Haven, CT: Yale University Press, 2010.

Badley, Kenneth Rea, and Harro W. Van Brummelen. *Metaphors We Teach By: How Metaphors Shape What We Do in Classrooms*. Eugene, OR: Wipf and Stock, 2012.

Briggs, Richard. *Reading the Bible Wisely*. Grand Rapids: Baker Academic, 2003.

Brueggemann, Walter. *The Creative Word: Canon as a Model for Biblical Education*. Philadelphia: Fortress, 1982.

Calvin, John. *Institutes of the Christian Religion*. Translated by Henry Beveridge. Grand Rapids: Christian Classics Ethereal Library, Calvin College, 1989. Online: http://www.ccel.org/ccel/calvin/institutes.html.

Clouser, Roy A. *The Myth of Religious Neutrality: An Essay on the Hidden Role of Belief in Theories*. Notre Dame, IN: Notre Dame University Press, 1991.

Comenius, John Amos. *The Great Didactic of John Amos Comenius*. Translated by M. W. Keatinge. London: A. & C. Black, 1896.

Egan, Kieran. *Teaching as Story Telling: An Alternative Approach to Teaching and Curriculum in the Elementary School*. London: Routledge, 1988.

Freire, Paulo. *Pedagogy of the Oppressed*. New York: Continuum, 1996.

Kidner, Derek. "Jesus the Teacher." *Religious Studies Today* 10 (1984) 9–12.

Klassen, Harold. "Visual Valet—Personal Assistant for Christian Thinkers and Teachers." Transforming Teachers. Online: http://www.transformingteachers.org/index.php?option=com_content&task=view&id=42&Itemid=142.

Lakoff, George, and Mark Johnson. *Metaphors We Live By*. Chicago: University of Chicago Press, 1980.

Lewis, C. S. *Mere Christianity*. San Francisco: HarperSanFrancisco, 2001.

MacIntyre, Alasdair. *After Virtue: An Essay in Moral Theory*. Notre Dame, IN: University of Notre Dame Press, 1984.

Makhado, Samson, and Dean Spalding. "Community and Hospitality in Multicultural Classrooms." *Journal of Education & Christian Belief* 5/2 (2001) 135–44.

Oliver, Gordon. *Holy Bible, Human Bible: Questions Pastoral Practice Must Ask*. Grand Rapids: Eerdmans, 2006.

Palmer, Parker J. *To Know as We are Known: A Spirituality of Education.* San Francisco: Harper & Row, 1983.

———. *The Courage to Teach: Exploring the Inner Landscape of a Teacher's Life.* San Francisco: Jossey Bass, 1998.

Peck, John, and Charles Strohmer. *Uncommon Sense: God's Wisdom for Our Complex and Changing World.* Sevierville, TN: Wise Press, 2000.

Pilger, Kathy D. and Ron Tagliapietra. *Algebra 1.* 2nd ed. Greenville, SC: BJU Press, 1999.

Postman, Neil. *The End of Education: Redefining the Value of School.* New York: Vintage, 1995.

Rutherford, Samuel. *The Loveliness of Christ: Extracts from the Letters of Samuel Rutherford.* Edited by Ellen S. Lister. Edinburgh: Banner of Truth Trust, 2007.

Ryken, Leland. *How to Read the Bible as Literature.* Grand Rapids: Zondervan, 1984.

Schön, Donald. "Generative Metaphor: A Perspective on Problem Setting in Social Policy." In *Metaphor and Thought,* edited by Andrew Ortony, 137–63. 2nd ed. Cambridge: Cambridge University Press, 1993.

Schwehn, Mark R. *Exiles from Eden: Religion and the Academic Vocation in America.* New York: Oxford University Press, 1993.

Shortt, John. "This Was a Real 'Aha!' Moment." True Stories of Transformation from the Classroom. European Educators' Christian Association Conference, 2009. Online: http://www.eureca-online.org/conferences/eureca conference2009/true-stories-of-transformation-from-the-classroom/this-was-a-real-aha-moment/.

Shortt, John, and John Westwell. *Charis Mathematics: Units 1–9.* St. Alban's, Hertfordshire: Association of Christian Teachers, 1996.

Smith, David I., and Barbara Carvill. *The Gift of the Stranger: Faith, Hospitality, and Foreign Language Learning.* Grand Rapids: Eerdmans, 2000.

Smith, David I., and John Shortt. *The Bible and the Task of Teaching.* Stapleford, Nottingham: Stapleford Centre, 2000.

Soskice, Janet Martin. *Metaphor and Religious Language.* Oxford: Clarendon, 1985.

Van Biema, David. "The Case for Teaching the Bible." *Time,* March 22, 2007. Online: http://content.time.com/time/magazine/article/0,9171,1601845,00.html.

Wilken, Robert Louis. "Going Deeper into the Bible: The Church Fathers as Interpreters." Lthe , Wheaton College, October 30, 2009. Audio recording. Online: http://espace.wheaton.edu/media/wetn/bith/mp3/091029wilken.mp3.

Wright, N. T. "How Can the Bible Be Authoritative?" *Vox Evangelica* 21 (1991) 7–32. Online: http://www.ntwrightpage.com/Wright_Bible_Authoritative.htm.

Wright, N. T. *The Last Word: Beyond the Bible Wars to a New Understanding of the Authority of Scripture.* New York: HarperCollins, 2005.

Subject Index

71

Name Index

Scripture Index

SCRIPTURE INDEX

Made in the USA
Lexington, KY
30 January 2016